Public Television in America

Public television in America

Public Television in America

Eli M. Noam
Jens Waltermann
(eds.)

Bertelsmann Foundation Publishers
Gütersloh 1998

Die Deutsche Bibliothek – CIP-Einheitsaufnahme
Public television in America : Eli M. Noam; Jens Waltermann (eds.). –
Gütersloh: Bertelsmann Foundation Publ., 1998
   ISBN 3-89204-388-4

© 1998 Bertelsmann Foundation Publishers, Gütersloh
Responsible: Jens Waltermann
Copy editor: Sabine Stadtfeld
Production editor: Kerstin Stoll
Cover design: HTG Werbeagentur, Bielefeld
Typesetting: digitron GmbH, Bielefeld
Print: Bonifatius GmbH, Druck · Buch · Verlag, Paderborn
ISBN 3-89204-388-4

Contents

Public Television: Past Promises and Future
Opportunities – an Introduction 7

The Institution of U.S. Public Broadcasting 11
Willard D. Rowland, Jr.

Funding and Economics of American Public Television 73
James Ledbetter

American Public Television:
Programs – Now, and in the Future 95
Richard Somerset-Ward

Public Television and New Technologies 113
Monroe E. Price

Public-Interest Programming by
American Commercial Television 145
Eli M. Noam

The Authors 177

Public Television: Past Promises and Future Opportunities – an Introduction

In Europe, television began in a public format and public broadcasting defined the video medium. But in America, public television was created to fill the programming void left by commercial TV, and tolerated as a belated addition rather than as a co-equal. For decades commercial television was controlled by three networks, and their economic imperative led towards entertainment programming. Education, by default, was served by public television, always the weaker part of the broadcasting system in terms of resources and audience.

Money was only part of the problem. The other was organization and vision. During the 1980s, cable television expanded rapidly, and with it, private cable channels. Public TV largely missed out on the opportunity to enter the era of multichannel television.

Today, public television is again at a major crossroad. Technologically, digitalization, multicasting, and the Internet provide a new challenge. Institutionally, the structure of the entire system is under scrutiny. And financially, its long-term funding mechanism is less certain than ever.

To investigate these themes, the Columbia Institute for Tele-Information created a research project on the future of public broadcasting in America. The project was part of an international and comparative effort involving several countries, initiated and led by the Bertelsmann Foundation. Some of the themes of the American study deserve a brief introduction.

Organizational Structure. American public TV has been very diverse, with hundreds of independent stations serving local needs. Yet the same diversity is a source of weakness, inhibiting public television from becoming a focused national voice and an efficient institution.

The Corporation for Public Broadcasting (CPB) was created in 1967 to distribute federal funds and provide strategic services. CPB created PBS (the Public Broadcasting Service) and NPR (National Public Radio), each responsible for developing programming and distribution. This structure has not met all goals. Decentralization had its cost in terms of efficiency. And the tension between the national system and the local stations, and among the local stations, has been chronic.

This issue is addressed by Willard Rowland in his chapter *The Institution of American Public Television.* Rowland traces the history of the system and its organization, and suggests that major structural changes need to occur. These include the consolidation of national-level public broadcasting entities, a reduction of local stations, and a more centralized national programming production capacity. All this would make the American system resemble more its public broadcasting cousins in Europe, Canada, and Japan. The likelihood of adoption of these proposals is not great.

Funding. Rowland also deals with the funding issue. Congressional leaders periodically advocate budgetary cutbacks for public TV, claiming political bias and questioning the necessity of the institution. Rowland, in contrast, advocates a dramatically increased funding from the federal government. This could be done through a "public dividend" in which Congress would create a public-service telecommunications trust fund, developed via increased amounts of spectrum auction and license transfer fees. In turn, the commercial broadcasters would be further deregulated.

Increased federal funding is only part of the revenue effort. To raise money, public television has also increasingly adopted private television revenue models, such as sponsorship of programs, near-ad-

8

vertisements, and "strategic partnerships" with private companies. What have been the consequences? This is the question tackled by James Ledbetter, the author of "Made Possible By," a book on public television finance. His chapter, *Funding and Economics of American Public Television*, traces the history of American public television funding, its current financial makeup, and the implications of new media vis-a-vis its funding in the future. Ledbetter is critical about the long-term impact of the self-commercialization of public television.

Technology Reforms and Content. The digitalization of the broadcast spectrum may allow public television to reclaim its program niches by "multicasting" multiple program channels. Similarly, the Internet's increasing role as an avenue for transmitting and receiving information provides new opportunities. These themes are taken up by Richard Somerset-Ward. In his article *American Public Television: Programs – Now and in the Future*, he reminds us that the original goal and intent of public television centered around disseminating educational and public interest programming. He recommends an increasing role for the public TV institutions, with technology providing new opportunities. A more pessimistic tone is expressed by Monroe Price in the chapter *Public Television and New Technologies*. Price does not believe that a technologically reformed PBS will strengthen American public broadcasting, or that it can play an international role in the way the BBC does.

Content Competition from Private Television. The technological innovations of multi-channel TV have given viewers new options. To what extent do commercial channels offer programs that in the past were delivered by public TV?

Eli Noam's article, *Public Interest Programming by American Commercial Television*, tracks and quantifies the contribution of commercial TV to public interest type programs. Using data points from the past three decades (1969, 1985, and 1997), the results show huge growth in the commercial offerings of public interest programming, primarily by cable TV channels. Their viewership now surpasses that of public TV, their diversity is impressive, and their budgets are cumulatively large. It is not the vast wasteland of the past. But several program categories remain underserved by commercial TV media, such as educational programs for children and cultural performances. Also, at about $300 a year, the cost of cable service can be a deterrent. Even so, the increased program role of private broadcasters forces public TV to reassess its programming strategy.

In conclusion: Most of the authors, though spanning the spectrum of views, seem to be sympathetic to public TV in principle; yet they are also skeptical about its ability to transition to the new media environment. On the whole, a pessimistic tone prevails.

Acknowledgments. The project is part of an international effort initiated and led by the Bertelsmann Foundation. Booz Allen & Hamilton, with Dr. Klaus Mattern as the project leader and Thomas Kuenstner, provided the international comparison. At Columbia University, the program director was Eli Noam, professor of Finance and Economics and director of the Columbia Institute for Tele-Information, with the substantial support of Hedahne Chung, project manager. We also thank Devin Burnam, Kristen Turturro, Carla Legendre, C. Andy Newcomer, and James Parker. At the Bertelsmann Foundation, the overall project was supervised by Dr. Ingrid Hamm, Vice President Media Division, and managed by Jens Waltermann, Director Media Policy.

The Institution of U.S. Public Broadcasting

Willard D. Rowland, Jr.

Contents

Summary of main points 12
Introduction 14
1. A brief history of public broadcasting 15
2. International comparisons: different
   expectations and capacities 26
3. The major constraints in the U.S. 29
   3.1 Internal structural limitations 29
   3.2 Programming mandate: the matter of the public
       and the problem of popularity 34
   3.3 Issues of oversight and accountability 36
   3.4 The constraints of funding 40
       3.4.1 Tax-based funding 46
       3.4.2 Private funding 55
4. Summary: a proposal for structural and process changes . . . 59
   4.1 Consolidation of national organizations 60
   4.2 Consolidation of local organizations 62
   4.3 Dramatically increased funding 64
Conclusion 66
Bibliography 67

11

Summary of main points

- U.S. public policy for communications has always been dominated by the First Amendment and a highly individualistic, libertarian social and economic ideology of the marketplace.
- That world view led to a well-ingrained pattern of private ownership and commercial purpose for the U.S. press, media and telecommunications, long before broadcasting emerged.
- Those entrenched structures of belief and motivation militated against strong forms of governmental regulation and public service in U.S. broadcasting.
- As a hedge against certain limitations of the private enterprise approach, a neo-libertarian, fiduciary policy of regulation in the "public interest, convenience and necessity" was adopted early in U.S. broadcasting, in the belief it would temper the commercial imperatives and foster a wider range of services within the private system.
- That policy failed, providing regulation largely in the interest of the regulated industries and encouraging competition only in a relatively narrow range of largely mass entertainment programming forms; it also worked against the maintenance of the initial nonprofit and noncommercial interests in broadcasting and subsequently the establishment of any significantly large, well-funded public service enterprise.
- The only aspect of public service broadcasting that had even modest support in the U.S. for the first four decades of radio and television was for educational uses.
- From the outset, the structure and operating procedures of U.S. educational broadcasting were highly decentralized and localized, setting a pattern of diffuse programming authority and complexity that, along with little or no significant funding support, discouraged development of strong national public broadcasting services.
- Those patterns and history were notably different from the experiences in other industrialized, "first-world" societies, where broadcasting was perceived initially less as an institution of

commerce and more as an important element of culture, leading to the establishment of the public service approach at the core of national broadcasting policies, usually at the beginning.

- Dissatisfaction with the performance of private, commercial broadcasting in the U.S. led to the Public Broadcasting Act of 1967 and an emphasis on public (as opposed to educational) broadcasting, the establishment of new national funding and program service agencies and the appropriation of federal funding for public broadcasting.

- However, such measures remained small by comparison with national policies for public broadcasting abroad; to this day U.S. public radio and television remain weak appendages to the dominant private system of commercial broadcasting, cable and telecommunications.

- U.S. public broadcasting is constrained by relatively small amounts of funding, a restrictive program mandate (i.e., a mission for educational, high-culture, alternative service, but not for entertainment and popularity), weak notions of public service, strong habits of congressional oversight, relatively small amounts of program production, a highly complex set of organizational structures and program procedures, and increasing commercialization.

- Possible remedies for the current weaknesses in U.S. public broadcasting include articulation of a broader mission, consolidation of organizations at local and national levels, the provision of a wider array of distinctly differentiated program services, and dramatically increased funding.

- The increased funding plan would be part of a "public dividend" policy, in which Congress would create a public service telecommunications trust fund, to be built from substantially increased amounts of spectrum auction and license transfer fees in exchange for further deregulation of the private, commercial aspects of U.S. broadcasting and telecommunications.

Introduction

Public broadcasting in the United States is widely seen as an important component of the nation's media culture (Carnegie, 1987, 1979, Twentieth Century Fund Task Force, 1993). Its programming, and the terms of public support for it, are not without criticism; it has its detractors from both the right and the left (Horowitz, 1995; Jarvik, 1997; Ledbetter, 1997). On the whole, however, public broadcasting tends to be endorsed as a social good; American society is seen as being better off for having it, for its role in broadening the base of information, education, cultural experience and political discourse.

Frequently, however, and often without regard to political perspective, public broadcasting is also criticized for being difficult to understand and analyze. Few observers, even among its most ardent supporters, can readily describe and explain it. Its institutional structure and procedures are usually seen as overly complex, Byzantine, inefficient and, at best, highly cumbersome.

Whether merited or not, such criticism is often made without a full understanding of the extent of the history of public broadcasting and the way in which that legacy has dictated certain persistent patterns in the institution's organization and operating processes. It is the purpose of this article to relate some of that history, so as to better describe the key elements in public broadcasting's structure and the range of constraints upon it. The article will cover matters of public broadcasting's legal and policy heritage, its social and cultural mandates, and its funding and structural limitations. The article concludes with a series of modest recommendations for changing public broadcasting's funding, structure and programming goals.

1. A brief history of public broadcasting

The institutional structure and workings of U.S. public broadcasting, and the constraints on it, are a direct result of public policy decisions taken for U.S. broadcasting beginning in the 1920s. Those decisions in turn are related to a deeper history of American communications media and public policy for their relationship to government and the private sector.

Ownership and control of most U.S. communications were vested early and firmly in private hands and commercial purpose. Under the formal dictates of the First Amendment and by virtue of Enlightenment-era understandings of the role of the individual and of the relationship between private interests and government, the press, telegraphy, telephony and film each became the province of private ownership, to be financed by commercial, profit-oriented mechanisms. Technological and capital cost considerations ("natural monopoly") led to a system of public regulatory oversight of telegraphy and telephony, but those industries were never publicly owned, and in exchange for rate and service commitments they were guaranteed certain levels of return and economic stability.

Matters of concentration and monopoly across a wide range of U.S. industrial enterprise (e. g., railroads, finance and oil), led to antitrust legislation and the development of federal regulatory structures by the late nineteenth century (Schwartz, 1973; Horwitz, 1989). From time to time there had been proposals for more direct forms of public ownership or involvement in communications (U.S. Post Office Department, 1914), but they never had much currency in American policy thinking, and they were not seriously proposed at the time of the development of the legislation dealing with radio.

The initial radio legislation (Radio Act of 1912) proved inadequate in several respects, not the least of which were a) that the original model of radio use was one of point-to-point radio telegraphy and telephony, not mass audience broadcasting, b) the known, usable spectrum of the day was insufficient to provide all the frequency demand emerging in the 1920s, and c) there was no satisfactory discretionary standard for making licensing assignments among the growing number of competing applicants. There also were concerns about broadcasting's putative social power and influence that abetted the interest in providing regulatory oversight.

Major features of the Radio Act of 1927 therefore were to create a new authority to make licensing decisions, the Federal Radio Commission (FRC), and to provide it with a licensing standard, "the public interest, convenience and necessity," adopted from existing forms of administrative oversight in such areas as transportation, finance and commerce. As adapted for radio that pattern imposed a fiduciary responsibility upon broadcasters, licensing them to use the airwaves in return for public interest service. The law also, however, explicitly forbade the FRC from content regulation, except for matters of obscenity.

In general, then, the law reflected much of the central tendencies in early twentieth-century understandings of the relationship between private and public interests and approaches at the time to regulating commerce. It also reflected the overall belief in the appropriate dominance of private enterprise in most industrial and social sectors. The 1927 radio law was developed in the wake of a generation of antitrust reform and federal regulatory activity in which the ideology of a progressive, socially responsible private-enterprise economy had been successfully resuscitated. That belief system in the mid-1920s also had become closely associated with equally optimistic expectations about the positive values of commercial forms of modern, popular communication. As a result, throughout the decade before the Great Depression there was little support for fashioning radio under any other template. The assumption remained that there was such considerable identity between private and public interests in broadcasting that, as in the simple models of eighteenth-century libertarianism, the best public services would emerge in a largely unfettered private enterprise.

Therefore, although it was never explicitly stated in the new Radio Act, a strong underlying assumption among many of its proponents and a strong article of faith in its fiduciary standard, was that the public's interest in broadcasting would best be served by retaining ownership in private hands and permitting a relatively unfettered form of commercial use. In that respect the policy followed the general tendencies for private ownership already dominant in all forms of U.S. communication, whether regulated or not.

Occasionally doubts were expressed about such prospects, and there were even explicit attempts to develop alternative, noncommercial radio services, typically under the auspices of educational, religious, labor, civic or municipal government institutions (Blakely, 1979, pp. 53–54; Frost, 1937; McChesney, 1993, p. 14). But those concerns and institutional alternatives were at such odds with the predominant world view that they remained relatively weak and ineffectual during the crucial "ballyhoo" years of the 1920s, when the basic structure of American broadcasting was being erected. As a result, the 1927 law made no provision for supporting or developing noncommercial broadcasting, and much of the work of the new FRC also militated against the few existing public service efforts (Blakely, 1979, pp. 54–55; McChesney, 1993, pp. 18–37), reinforcing tendencies that even before 1927 had been discouraging educational and other noncommercial efforts (Barnouw, 1966, pp. 172–174).

During the early 1920s the emerging broadcasting industry had become dominated by large national interests in electrical manufacturing and telecommunications (e.g., General Electric, Westinghouse, AT&T, and their creation, the Radio Corporation of America). During the two years immediately preceding passage of the 1927 act, those interests, in conjunction with a proliferating number of local stations and the rapidly growing national advertising industry, had begun to create a system of national commercial networks and centralized program production. Following the syndication and chain logic of many other national industries including the press and film, RCA created the National Broadcasting Company (NBC), and negotiations among a shifting group of phonograph (Columbia), film (Paramount), and tobacco interests led to formation of the Columbia Broadcasting Company (CBS), both in 1926–1927. The new law barely took cognizance of those structures (Barnouw, 1966, pp. 198–200). In direct contrast to the emerging pattern abroad it provided for licensing only of the local stations, not of the national networks. Its overall approach was to imagine and to try to assure that control of the system would be vested in local hands, and it did not address either the power of the network imperative or the implicit tension between the increasingly central role of advertising support and the fiduciary standard.

During the early 1930s, as the Depression deepened and a broader debate raged about appropriate economic and social reforms, there emerged a certain degree of dissatisfaction with the limited extent of public service in commercial radio (Blakely, 1979, pp. 55–64). Many educational institutions, particularly land-grant colleges and universities, continued to try to develop a separate system of educational stations, and to support that effort, they sought legislation attempting to reserve AM frequency space for noncommercial or nonprofit licensees.

But by the mid-1930s, such statutory efforts, most notably the proposed Wagner-Hatfield amendment to the 1934 Communications Act, had failed (Blakely, 1979, pp. 64–66; McChesney, 1993, pp. 196–210). As a result of the Depression and the discriminatory spectrum reallocation and other licensing policies of the FRC, many public agencies and private nonprofit institutions had withdrawn from radio operations (frequently selling out to commercial interests). With the number of active stations drastically reduced, the opportunity for much noncommercial production and for audiences to experience it were concomitantly lessened. In the absence of any major alternatives the public was increasingly cultivated with the light-entertainment forms of commercial radio. Meanwhile, the industry was making considerable claims about its intentions of working with noncommercial interests to offer alternative educational and high-cultural programming, and indeed for a period it actually seemed to be doing so. The educational leaders were themselves divided over how thoroughly separate a system of broadcasting was necessary. Simultaneously, whatever else the Roosevelt administration was accomplishing through its New Deal programs, it was not contemplating any significant restructuring of the U.S. broadcasting system.

Throughout this period a small group of noncommercial stations, largely at state colleges and universities, did survive, and eventually, by the late 1930s, the Federal Communications Commission (FCC) had set aside reserved frequencies for exclusive use by such entities. But those reservations had come late, they were only in the new, as

18

yet unavailable FM band, and they were never extended back into the then predominant AM band. Further, they were preserved for a limited class of stations – "noncommercial educational." The name evoked something far less popular, much more local and considerably less universal than the concept of national public-service broadcasting being developed abroad. This form of radio in the U.S. was seen to be necessary only in a relatively restricted domain of instructional, formally pedagogic service. Its models were principally those of the classroom – the lecture, the textbook and the training film. Only fitfully did it dwell in the realms of drama, public affairs or the popular. It was merely an alternative, at best a minor, secondary service with tiny resources and few public expectations that it should be anything more. It also was not seen as a national, integrated enterprise.

As a result during the heyday of American AM radio (1927–1955) noncommercial licensees had almost no presence in the medium, particularly in large population centers. There was no national, interconnected public service network, no national production capacity, no federal funding and a set of other revenues that remained minuscule by any standard abroad. With this poor heritage the noncommercial radio service was so narrowly defined, so locally based, and so technologically limited that well into the 1970s it was barely audible in U.S. media culture.

By the time of World War II, as the economy was beginning to recover and international political crises stimulated wider debate about the meaning and health of American democracy, certain contradictions in U.S. mass media structures and practices had become somewhat more apparent. The inconsistencies between the promises of libertarian expectations for the several mass media and their actual performances were discussed in the report of the Hutchins Commission, 1943–1946 (Commission on Freedom of the Press, 1947). More specific critiques of the radio industry were rendered in a special Hutchins Commission study, the White report (1947), and in a parallel, though unconnected, FCC staff report, the Blue Book (FCC, 1946). All three documents were couched in terms of what was becoming known as the social-responsibility theory of the press and media behavior (Peterson, 1956) in which the failures of private, commercially sponsored, profit-driven media institutions were decried and recommendations for improved public service were issued. The Blue Book seemed to be laying the groundwork for stricter FCC regulation of public service performance by commercial licensees, and the Hutchins recommendations, supported by the critical White analysis, actually included provisions for a stronger noncommercial broadcasting effort and the introduction of federal government support.

However, neither the Blue Book nor the Hutchins report was ever adopted as official policy. They were too controversial, too explicitly threatening to the existing private enterprise interests and free-expression mythologies. They therefore had no immediate effect on basic terms of communication ownership, purpose, and control. The social-responsibility theory was capable of sharp criticism, but as an essentially neo-libertarian construct it had little capacity for significantly affecting public and political attitudes about major, necessary structural changes. It was a creature of the progressive, liberal reform ideology that had been fostering precisely the failures and contradictions that it was criticizing, and it never could transcend that dilemma (Nerone, 1995). Despite mounting evidence to the contrary, the public interest was still thought to reside in an overwhelmingly private, commercial system tempered by the existing form of federal regulation. Public-service communication values and institutions were never widely understood in the broader British, European, and Canadian terms. Indeed the public service organizations abroad tended to be seen, and dismissed, as "state" broadcasting. It remained an article of faith that whatever weaknesses there were in the United States, they could be overcome in time through the workings of enlightened, public-spirited, private broadcasting leadership, moderate FCC oversight, and the introduction of yet another, newer electronic technology.

In this light it is clearer why U.S. television also developed in a way that, patterned after radio, provided only a small space for formal institutionalization of a public-service effort, and never along the lines of anything approaching the models abroad. The core structure of commercial network radio was almost immediately replicated in the new television industry with many of the same local and large national private interests taking charge of the new medium. Congress provided for no new statutory framework for television, and the FCC's approach was one of essentially endorsing that mapping of the radio structure and commercial logic onto television. By 1952 the NBC and CBS television networks were well in place and a burgeoning system of local network affiliates was emerging. ABC, the product of a regulatively imposed divestiture of one of NBC's previous two radio networks, was struggling, and one or two other networks failed in the mid-1950s. But the basic pattern was well-established early on and the general policy that had been formed nearly thirty years earlier during the origins of radio remained intact as television emerged.

For the next twenty years the structure of U.S. commercial television remained largely the same. The system was dominated by the three networks, which, with a loose array of independent stations across the country provided four to six channels in most major cities. The networks were made up of a combination of stations which they owned and operated, five to seven each, usually in large cities, plus dozens of affiliate stations owned by others, but contractually linked to one of the networks for the provision of an exclusive program service. Those services were a mixture of program types – news, sports, film and a large amount of popular entertainment. The entire structure was supported by advertising, national and local, and as a result the three major networks tended to resemble one another with similar mixtures of program types. Unlike the national channels in other countries they were not programmed to be different from another or complementary. But due to their exclusive advertising source of revenue they were designed to be competitive with one another in each of the program content areas.

There always were some reservations about the true diversity of content and service reflected in such a system, and that is why there was some support in the early 1950s for at least a modest educational alternative. But the notion of a major, well-funded public service alternative was not part of the policy debates in the early years. Therefore the ETV service that was developing through the 1950s and mid-1960s was a weak appendage of the major national, commercial structure.

By the mid-1970s cable television had begun to be an increasingly important part of the U.S. system of broadcasting. Originally cable had been an unconnected collection of local community antenna television systems (CATV), retransmitting local and nearby television stations for communities which, due to geographic location, had difficulty receiving the signals off-air. Such systems were typically isolated from one another, offering 6-12 channels each, and independently owned. With the advent of broader-band coaxial cable and a permanent, reliable, geostationary satellite delivery mechanism, cable was able to provide considerably more channels (20-36), including a set of national program services (film, sports, and even local independent stations), and they were becoming aggregated in multiply owned systems (MSOs) that in turn were assimilating themselves into the national entertainment and cultural industry system, with cross ownership interests in film, video production, news and sports franchises.

Geared to the regulation of broadcasting and the common carrier telecommunications industries, the FCC had been highly protectionist of the existing commercial television system as cable began to develop. A series of government and private studies and court actions helped change the Commission's posture, and by the mid-1970s cable was no longer being discriminated against. In fact, over time, cable was successful in achieving a highly privileged regulatory status independent both of common carriers and broadcasting. It avoided the rate and service regulation policies for telecommunications, while also being exempted from the public-interest licensing obligations of broadcasters. Deregulation was the hallmark of federal regulation for communications by the late-1970s; by the time of the Cable Communications Act of 1984 it had become the dominant theme of federal policy for cable. Meanwhile, deregulation continued in broadcasting, with the elimination of such central tenets as the Fairness Doctrine (FCC, 1987) and aspects of the cross ownership rules.

However all this change in federal policy for commercial broadcasting and cable had few implications for public-service television in the U.S. Educational television earned a certain degree of official support in the early 1950s, when for instance, the FCC provided frequency reservations for noncommercial stations. This reservation policy was adopted earlier in the history of television than it had been in radio, preserving a somewhat broader initial niche. But, again, the concept of television in this realm was strictly limited, and the practical resources to realize anything more were not there. To its academic, philanthropic, state educational, and private, high-cultural constituencies, noncommercial television was more exciting than educational radio and therefore, from the outset, it did attract more substantial support locally and nationally than had educational radio. Yet, that support still tended to view this form of television in restricted terms. Its very name, ETV, evoked the old problem of "noncommercial educational" broadcasting. It was to be a service that was only a secondary alternative to the dominant private-commercial enterprise, with little or none of the expectations of popularity, universal service and wide-ranging subject matter associated with public television elsewhere. There remained a strong belief that private-enterprise, commercially-supported television would provide enough to satisfy the public so that no other option need be addressed. As before, the belief was that any failures that might emerge in the commercial realm could be corrected by appeals to private broadcasters' consciences, gentle regulatory coercion, and an ETV service supported at minimal levels, largely by local interests, universities, and state authorities.

Furthermore, any tendency to question such assumptions or to invoke other public service models from abroad could be little advanced during the early Cold War/McCarthy era. That environment fostered jingoistic appeals to the most simplistic images of what was right and just in American values and institutions, and it trafficked in fear of anything alien or foreign, especially in such sensitive areas as communication, with all its overtones of concern about propaganda and freedom. Altogether then, almost no one, including the noncommercial interests themselves, were articulating a vision of a large, wide-ranging public service television institution that would be more central to U.S. broadcasting culture than educational radio had been.

The weaknesses of the commercial-adequacy assumption were sufficiently apparent by the late 1960s that federal policy for broadcasting began to institutionalize certain adjustments. Federal support had moved beyond providing reserved frequencies to funding a few forms of instructional programming (1958) and the construction of noncommercial facilities (1962).[1] Now, particularly in the wake of the Carnegie Commission report of 1967 (Carnegie-I), the government was bringing itself to the point of beginning to provide funds for more general programming, national systems of public radio and television interconnection, and other grants for local licensees to use at their discretion. That apparently changing federal policy reflected the interest among various national centers of private and public power and among many state governments and associated local private interests in increasing the number of public television and radio facilities. Simultaneously, the more substantial federal initiative stimulated the state and local tendencies, with the result that the Public Broadcasting Act of 1967 helped lead to the creation of a larger, more powerful national-level superstructure, including the Corporation for Public Broadcasting (CPB), the Public Broadcasting Service (PBS), and National Public Radio (NPR); a proliferation of public stations; stronger regional activities; more hours of national programming; and a more widely available and attended range of services.

The change in name and status signaled a certain broadening of purpose and potential service; it seemed to be stating the case for a substantially refurbished and upgraded public-service enterprise. There were wider expectations that public broadcasting should reach more people, address more interests, and generally elevate the quality of electronic media discourse. This was a trend that had begun in the mid-1950s, with the widening institutional basis of ETV licensee organizations in response to the expanding range of interests in noncommercial television's use. Various philanthropies, industrial interests, and other cultural organizations at the local level, most typi-

---

1 The initial reservations (12 percent of all television allocations) were included in the FCC's Sixth Report and Order (1952); the instructional television support, for $3 million to $5 million a year for research and experimentation in broadcasting and film, was in Title VII of the National Defense Education Act; and the construction funds, for up to 50 percent of the total cost of projects – initially only in television, not radio – were authorized by the Educational Television Facilities Act of 1962. See Blakely, (1979), pp. 89–93, 135, 143–144.

fied nationally by the Ford Foundation, had organized "community licensees" and had influenced other more traditional educational interests to encourage all forms of ETV stations to produce and carry a range of programming that was less formally instructional in nature. Efforts in drama, music, children's programming, and even public affairs began to be introduced with a broader, more general audience in mind. Such trends were particularly encouraged through the Ford-supported national production and distribution center, National Education Television (NET), from the mid-1950s to the late 1960s (Jones and Rowland, 1990).

Meanwhile, during the 1960s and 1970s, licensee governance broadened to include a wider range of citizenry – leaders and representatives of an expanding realm of professional and social interests. Community group and state telecommunications authority licensees became increasingly prominent in local and national public broadcasting affairs, while local school district licensees actually declined. Although the number of university and state educational authority licensees increased, their boards, advisory committees, and managements tended to reflect a broader, less strictly educational orientation. These changes accelerated after the 1967 Public Broadcasting Act, which introduced additional federal funding and attracted attention to and support for noncommercial radio and television as a national enterprise, a public broadcasting "system." But as important as all these developments were, they were slow in coming, and they either papered over old tensions and problems or introduced new ones.

The remainder of this article will review the principal issues involving public broadcasting's programming mandate, its structure, its relationship to government and the overall question of its independence. It will introduce that discussion by reviewing certain differences between the characteristics of public broadcasting in the U.S. and the predominant patterns elsewhere.

2. International comparisons: different expectations and capacities

In addition to the deep policy history outlined above, another way of understanding the structural and operating conditions of U.S. public broadcasting is to compare its mandate and status to its counterpart entities abroad. There is now sufficient research on public broadcasting in the U.S. and other societies to make it possible to outline and evaluate the contrasts among national communication policies, public service media structures and funding patterns around the world, e.g., Avery (1993), Blumler (1989), Browne (1989), Day (1995), Engleman (1996), Fox (1997), Hoffman-Riem (1996), Lewis and Booth (1990), Rowland and Tracey (1990), Somerset-Ward (1993).

The details of national policy for public broadcasting vary considerably from country to country. But among most industrialized, "first world" democracies there are certain characteristics or tendencies in the arrangements for public broadcasting that are telling departures from the situation in the U.S.

Public broadcasting abroad has historically been far more central to broadcasting and telecommunications cultures.
In most instances the public-service institutions were built first; the commercial and private elements came later. As a result, the broadcast programming cultures in those nations tend to be defined by and revolve around the public-service ethic, rather than the other way around.

Broadcasting in other advanced societies is seen primarily as a cultural institution and only secondarily as an economic enterprise.
The primacy of the public-service ethos elsewhere derives from the tendency to understand broadcasting first as a matter of language, symbols, meaning, social identity and cultural expression. In the U.S. broadcasting historically has been seen primarily as a business, as an engine of and actor in commerce.

Public broadcasting abroad tends to continue to be supported much more richly by public funds on a per capita basis.
This condition has remained true in virtually all other countries, even in an era of increasing privatization and commercialization. The public broadcasting funding disparities between those countries and the U.S. continue to be of large magnitude and to lead to dramatically different programming possibilities.

Nationally chartered public-service broadcasting corporations (PSBCs) tend to produce much larger amounts of programming.
Most PSBCs have the budgets, facilities, staffs and mandates to produce large volumes of programs on a regular basis, day in and day out. As a result they tend to be able to provide a steady stream of high-quality material with considerably more regularity than in the U.S.

PSBCs abroad also tend to provide multiple strands of complementary national program services.
Most PSBC service mandates are quite broad, such that they are expected to provide a rich array of programming for both general and specialized audiences. The structural consequence of that expectation is that the PSBCs organize their programming in several coherent streams of separately identifiable services. Such services are universally available and delivered as distinct channels or networks.

The PSBC missions are so comprehensive that they are expected to be both popular and entertaining for the entire public in at least some aspects of their services.
Most national public broadcasters derive their current missions and roles – "to inform, educate and entertain" – from the original BBC charter (Briggs, 1961, pp. 348–360). By contrast in the U.S., the issue of entertainment is severely circumscribed by the dominant commercial system. There are concerns abroad about pandering to simple tastes, but in most such countries public broadcasting's right, indeed its responsibility, to be entertaining is usually quite clear. The special contribution of public-service broadcasting insofar as popularity is concerned is to attend to matters of quality, to explore

the extent to which it is possible to have widespread popular appeal while yet striving to provide information, education and general enlightenment.

Where public radio and television are managed together in one organization they tend to have synergies that improve both.
Radio and television are different media. But public radio and public television share a common public service ethic that binds them more tightly than to their respective private counterparts. Under that joint banner the two media have the potential of working together more effectively. In those instances abroad where they share the same corporate charter they tend to be able to pool objectives and resources with far better results in public appreciation, policy development, programming and administrative efficiencies.

The number of public-service institutions in other countries tend to be far fewer, making it possible for them to be more coherent, focused and effective in their policy representations.
Most frequently there is only one principal public broadcasting organization in each society abroad. There seldom are more than two or three. As a result the public relations and national lobby energies are much more focused and less subject to multiple interpretations by the public and other parties. Such unity makes public service broadcasting much less subject to the divisiveness encouraged by hostile political and private forces.

This is not to suggest that public broadcasting abroad is without problems. In various systems there are difficulties associated with politicization, over-commercialization, and inefficient use of resources. In some countries there also have been serious episodes of self doubt and loss of vision and commitment (Rowland and Tracey, 1990). But on the whole there has been much more effective attention abroad to how public broadcasting can work positively in the development and maintenance of national and regional cultures, public voices and civic identity.

The difficulty for public broadcasting in the U.S. is that it has all the problems of its counterparts abroad with few of the advantages.

It has little consensus on just what is its mission, it is subject to considerable political pressure due to the particular mechanisms of its federal funding arrangement, it remains profoundly underfunded and therefore underproductive, and it is becoming increasingly commercial.

3. The major constraints in the U.S.

3.1 Internal structural limitations

The policy history outlined in Section I above depicts how at the outset, with the emphasis on supporting a private, commercial system and investing in the faith that such a system would provide a diverse body of public services, there was virtually no support for federal funding or building a major national public service programming and distribution enterprise, in either radio or television. As a result, U.S. public broadcasting grew up around a weak collection of independent local educational licensee organizations (universities, community groups, school boards and state educational authorities). Over the decades U.S. public broadcasting has been fashioned in a crazy-quilt structure that cannot be readily explained. Its structural origins are first Jeffersonian and then Madisonian. In theory the results seem to have all the benefits of the Federalist compromises, of both vertical and horizontal checks and balances. In practice the structure is severely restrictive.

The Jeffersonian aspects of the structure, the "state's rights" elements, came into being in the 1930s and were firmly entrenched by the mid-1960s with the emergence of the first Carnegie report (1967) and the Public Broadcasting Act of 1967. Those characteristics had been rationalized around the principle of local control of programming and concerns about the putatively overweening power of national centers of programming production and distribution. The use of the word "network," for instance, early became anathema in public broadcasting. The local licensees had formed a national organization, the National Association of Educational Broadcasters (NAEB), that among other things had programming divisions, National Educational Radio (NER) and Educational Television Stations (ETS) (Blakely, 1979). But as membership controlled entities with no major federal or private funding, neither of those agencies had significant programming development resources or authority.

National Educational Television (NET) was the only other major national program service before 1967. Its acronym suggested the ambition of becoming a full-fledged broadcasting network, and to a certain extent by comparison with the NAEB divisions, it was. But even NET, with a steady funding stream from the Ford Foundation, was a modest program service; at its height in the late-1960s it provided only about ten hours of programming each week, and it never had a permanent interconnection capacity.

With the social turmoil of the late 1960s, it became politically difficult to argue for a centralized model such as the British, Canadian or Japanese Broadcasting Corporations. Many local communities and the stations serving them felt that NET was part of an "Eastern, liberal political establishment" that they perceived already to be well-represented in the commercial television networks. That NET was centered in New York and benefited from the nearly exclusive support of the Ford Foundation only reinforced the impression of many around the country and in Congress that a more decentralized program model was necessary when federal support became available after 1967 (Day, 1995).

As a result, in public television the new Corporation for Public Broadcasting (CPB), in league with the existing public television stations, agreed to a model for the new interconnection service (PBS) that denied it the right either to produce programs itself or to operate independently (Avery and Pepper, 1980). From the outset PBS was to be a membership organization, subject to the broad-ranging and often conflicting interests of its members. It also was designed to rely almost exclusively on its members for programming. This was at some variance with the situation in radio, where NPR, the new counterpart to PBS, was invested with a good deal of centralized program authority and was permitted to produce programs itself. The television situation also stood in stark contrast to that of public broadcasting abroad, where centralized national public service networks, complete with large staffs of production talent, were the norm.

The differences in this regard between radio and television were the result of different strengths among their stations. One of public radio's weaknesses became a strong argument for giving program production authority to NPR. Prior to 1967 there were few educational radio stations with the production expertise necessary to mount a daily schedule of consistently high quality public service radio programs for national audiences. The new NPR would therefore have little competition for national production rights and resources, at least initially. By contrast in educational television, several stations, in addition to NET, had developed national production capacity. Loosely known as the "six pack" (Avery and Pepper, 1980) they had already been struggling with NET for rights to produce for the national service. In league with the broader base of local ETV stations, they successfully argued against allowing the new PBS, which they largely controlled as an owners' cooperative, from having production authority, forcing it to carry their programs instead.

Perhaps the most striking feature of the national public broadcasting arrangement in the U.S. was that unlike the nationally chartered public service corporations elsewhere, CPB itself was thoroughly constrained in its role. The 1967 act prevented CPB from becoming either a program producer or program distributor. It could establish national intercommunication systems and it could fund public service programming, but it could not make such programs itself, nor own or operate national services fashioned around them.

From the outset of the post-Carnegie period, then, the normal functions of national public broadcasting were divided among CPB, PBS, NPR, the stations and other entities. The situation was particularly cumbersome in television, where PBS was limited to a role of providing technical interconnection among the PTV stations and coordinating the program schedule for them. That initial anti-federal model for public television was reinforced during the mid-1970s, in the wake of presidential interference in the media, including public television (Day, 1995). The PBS governance structure was adjusted to reinforce its fundamental characteristic of station membership ownership and control. That tendency in turn led to the design and implementation in 1974 of the Station Program Cooperative (SPC), a mechanism whereby federal funds for programming were passed through to the stations and pooled for particular program projects as proposed from among the many different producing entities. That system proved to be highly cumbersome and lacking in creativity, as it assigned no real editorial accountability and generally favored those proposals that provided more hours for less cost.

In 1990 public television abandoned the SPC mechanism, in an attempt to concentrate more funding and central program commissioning authority in PBS. But to this day the funds available for that process remain paltry by comparison with other national public television organizations. PBS, unlike NPR, still has no production authority itself. The producers for national public television continue to be associated with a handful of large stations or state networks that compete with one another for the few funding crumbs that are available. It is a highly erratic, disjointed system that is in a constant state of flux and that provides no stability for the vast majority of producers and related production talent. As a result national public television programming continues to be small in quantity and limited in quality. While major productions across a wide range of topics are produced daily and weekly in other national public television systems, they are few and far between in the U.S. To be sure, certain national programs in both public radio and television are produced regularly, and a few even daily. But they constitute only a fraction of the regular, daily programming provided by the public-service corporations in most other democracies.

A myriad of organizations at national, regional and local levels all compete for scarce program funding, and yet few of them are strong enough to sustain such efforts on a regular basis. Even among those that do, the resulting amount of program production is relatively small. The typical pattern of U.S. public television production is one in which individual efforts are mounted for a particular program or series, only to be disbanded at the conclusion of the project. Each new program effort then requires a wholly new, separate funding and production cycle, wherein talent has to be reaggregated, often with considerable loss of time and creative energy. At the end of the project the team typically dissipates once again. Very few public television programs and production entities have had a consistent, steady source of adequate revenue. As a result U.S. television is forced to approach much of its production responsibility as an ad hoc, intermittent process.

By comparison abroad, public-service broadcasting in virtually every other industrialized democracy has strong, deeply resourced, national program production capacities. While the exact details vary considerably from nation to nation, the principle remains the same. In virtually every case there are large concentrations of program production funds, facilities and people permanently organized around the public service program mission. With the arguable exception of public radio and a few continuing public television programs, public broadcasting in the U.S. has little of that characteristic.

Most of the separate public broadcasting organizations also compete with one another for the right to speak on behalf of the institution, and as a result, policy planning for public television and radio is almost nonexistent. With all its diverse power bases public broadcasting tends to be reactive to external political agendas. It has almost no capacity for setting its sights on long-term objectives that provide for its growth and development and an ever increasing centrality in American cultural life. Public broadcasting's recent failure to establish any position for itself in the Telecommunications Act of 1996 is a telling case in point. In no other country could so sweeping and important a piece of communications legislation be debated, let alone pass, without a full-fledged hearing of the case for the public service media. That such a debate did not occur in the recent legislative process is a mark of the marginality with which public broadcasting is perceived in the U.S. and of its own internal incapacity to work effectively to articulate a vision for the public-service concept.

3.2 Programming mandate: the matter of the public and the problem of popularity[2]

When Carnegie-I (1967) invoked the term *public*, it was clearly trying to create a new image for the enterprise. It could not dismiss entirely the educational label, for too much policy support at the local, state, and federal levels had been built on the assumption of the inherent worth of the association with education. However, Carnegie did try to transcend the issue by incorporating broad notions of general audience service and high production quality that would earn much wider funding support from private and public sources, while yet retaining enough of the traditional educational values to qualify legitimately as something other than conventional, commercial television.

Widely though not universally supported within public broadcasting, this approach did much to improve the attractiveness of the service to the broad moderate center of U.S. political and cultural tastes. But that very condition led to an increasing dilemma: the contradictions of popularity and publicness. For as noncommercial broadcasting had begun to call itself "public" and to use that title to justify calls for increased federal and state funds, it also had begun to be asked whether it ought not to be able to demonstrate a considerably wider audience reach on a more frequent basis. Yet at the same time, it was vulnerable to charges of trying to be too popular ("commercial") and also being too unaccountable to the public now providing it more support.

The popularity matter was, and remains, awkward. If more tax-based resources were to be dedicated to public broadcasting, should not it be both more universally available and more attractive to larger, even majority audiences, as with public broadcasting elsewhere? The technical problem of inadequate and unavailable signals could be overcome with more federal and state construction money. But what then? Should public broadcasting be expected to attract more of that newly available audience, and if so, how? Could public attention be increased through programming or services targeted to vari-

2 Portions of sections III B-D are drawn from Rowland (1993).

34

ous special social, ethnic, and economic groups or through material of more general audience appeal? But then, by whatever means it might be becoming more popular, how would it avoid charges of engaging in ratings' competition? If successful in building popular new program services, how would it adjust to charges of depressing the revenues of private broadcasters? How would it respond to losing some of its programs to the commercial marketplace, and would it generally manage to maintain a separate, supportable identity?

On the one hand, there was concern about whether public broadcasting was not going to be popular enough, whether it would remain the province of educational and cultural elites and therefore unworthy of public funds whatsoever, let alone substantial increases. On the other hand, there was concern that it would become too popular, becoming indistinct from the conventional commercial services, and in the process drawing so much audience and profitability from them that it would threaten the as yet fragile national policy consensus supporting its relatively recent elevation to a somewhat higher order of activity, presence, and status.

The problem has been exacerbated in the U.S. by virtue of the restrictions on public broadcasting's mandate for entertainment. Commercial broadcasting makes a strong claim for its primacy in that regard, and because the entertainment function was ingrained in the commercial realms well before public broadcasting began to achieve a post-Carnegie national mandate, the notion of public television's role as only a secondary, largely educational "alternative" was little questioned. With a few arguable exceptions (Carnegie II, 1979; Rowland and Tracey, 1991) the debate in the U.S. has never been able to address the linkages among entertainment, popularity and quality so well developed abroad. The notion that there could be a public-service mandate to bring quality into the popular and thereby improve the tenor of a wide range of television, and that to do so would require the establishment of large-scale, exceedingly well-funded noncommercial programming institution, has never been widely understood in the U.S.

3.3 Issues of oversight and accountability

The idea of publicness also had introduced difficult questions about governance, access, and accountability. Such questions would have arisen in general form with the introduction of any significant amount of federal funding for programming. They are endemic issues for all democratic societies that provide public support for broadcasting, the arts, theater or any activity involving communication and speech. Insofar as U.S. public broadcasting is concerned, these issues emerged amid the 1960s and 1970s debates about the redistribution of power throughout U.S. society and its institutions – the basic concerns about democratization in the struggles over civil rights, Vietnam, consumerism, and the environment, as well as all the issues involving the role of the government in many social institutions as reflected in such matters as education, welfare, affirmative action and the "culture wars."

In that context, noncommercial broadcasting found that it could not claim to be public and yet avoid scrutiny about its responsibilities to that public. To accept more tax-generated funding, especially at the federal level, was to invite inquiry into its criteria and mechanisms for choosing governing boards and managements, for determining necessary services, and for supporting particular programming. Educational broadcasting had long been exempt from concerns about accountability. Its public funding had been minuscule (and nonexistent at the federal level), and it had, after all, been fostered primarily in the halls of higher education, where considerations of academic freedom and protection from intense, direct, public scrutiny usually prevailed. As an educationally high-minded or "uplift" activity, noncommercial broadcasting had also been accustomed to the benefit of the doubt about its social responsibilities – to a presumption of inherent goodwill, progressivism, and general improvement over what existed in the commercial realm. Consequently, public broadcasting was not initially well prepared for charges of discrimination, elitism and fiscal irresponsibility.

Few public broadcasters or their principal policy supporters seemed to be able to put these concerns into any historical perspective. In all the commentary and research on public broadcasting published in the period between Carnegies I and II (1967–1979) there was virtually no recognition of the depth of the problem of public-ness, no apparent awareness of the rich arguments about it stretching back through American history, with particularly acute expressions in the early twentieth-century debates about pragmatism and pro-gressivism (Lippmann, 1922; Dewey, 1927). Broadcasters and pub-lic policymakers seemed to have little or no knowledge of these ar-guments and about how they might bear on contemporary struggles over the new media. Demonstrating a relatively shallow social and political consciousness about this institution they were building, public broadcasters had few tools for understanding how serious, and not merely partisan and special-interest-based, were many of the questions being raised about its publicness.

As a result, when such questions became a more regular part of the policy debates in the mid- and late 1970s, many public broad-casting responses, as expressed in board meetings, national confer-ences, and political lobbying, were fearful and defensive, appearing to be insensitive and even reactionary. There was such resistance to inquiries about governance, accountability, and access that many of the generally friendly forces in the policymaking arena were dis-comfited. Many public broadcasters took it for granted that it would be understood that they were providing participation for diverse in-terests, particularly for those that had historically been underrepre-sented in U.S. broadcasting, and they assumed that appropriate cred-it would accrue to the institution for such efforts. Yet they found, often to their consternation, that public interest groups, minority and feminist spokespersons, independent producers, and others were be-ginning to suggest that public broadcasting was too inbred, too re-flective of a white, male, upper-middle class outlook that was much more closely associated with established, unprogressive forces in the social and economic order than it realized and hence, that substantial alterations in policy for funding and oversight were necessary.

That particular criticism became institutionalized in the form of increasingly organized efforts by local citizen activist groups and, particularly, independent producers. The national program develop-ment policies worked out by CPB, PBS, and the stations during the 1970s heavily favored submissions from the existing stations, particularly larger "community" licensees in the major cities that had built substantial production plants. Writers and producers unaffiliated with such stations, and therefore independent of their managements, boards, and funding structures, had almost no access to the federally provided production funds channeled through CPB or to the national schedule controlled by PBS and its member stations.

In response to this situation, many of the independent producers and associated nonstation interests began to call for changes in the structure of national program funding. By at least the time of the 1978 Public Telecommunications Financing Act, the influence of these groups was being felt and reflected in Congress. Some accommodations were made during the early and mid-1980s, but the independent producer community continued to feel that the program funding process was still stacked too systematically against it. Accordingly, through a steady process of representations before CPB and PBS, as well as a few major stations, the independents continued to organize themselves and achieve even more sympathetic hearings in Congress. Their efforts were parallel to, if not strictly modeled on, a similar set of activities abroad. Most other public broadcasting establishments had also come under fire for allegedly restricting production and programming practices, and those disputes had led to significant changes in national broadcast policies. Perhaps the most notable of these was the debate in Britain over the concept of the proposed Open Broadcast Authority and the eventual creation instead of Channel 4 (Blanchard and Morley, 1982).

In the United States the independent efforts achieved a somewhat less dramatic but nonetheless unprecedented success when in 1988, as part of a new federal reauthorization bill, CPB was forced to set aside portions of its funds for the support of independent program efforts (Public Telecommunications Act of 1988). The new law also directed CPB to create and fund a new independent production service. The result was the formation in 1989 of a formal organization, the Independent Television Service (ITVS), that would coordinate program grants to nonstation producers to expand program diversity and innovativeness and thereby, presumably, to foster a wider range of program voices within the public-television community (*Broadcasting*, 1989; Drickey, 1989).

A similar set of tensions has prevailed between much of public broadcasting and the public-access movement in cable television. Public television stations have tended to view community-access producers with suspicion and disdain, as highly self-interested, partisan spokespersons for special causes with little production and program sophistication. To this day there are few production alliances between community-access interests and public television.[3] For their part the former tend to perceive the latter as being too little committed to fundamental issues of democracy and community action and still too beholden to liberal-centrist ideologies of pluralism, high culture and accommodation with economic and social power.

Meanwhile, from quite opposite, more conservative directions public broadcasting has continued to be accused of being, in fact, too immoderate, too "liberal," if not leftist, and too much a part of that coalition of old New Deal and recent Great Society forces that had been characterized as undermining traditional U.S. economic and spiritual values. It also has been seen to be contributing to an overly large, stifling, and inflationary public sector and, like the National Endowments for the Arts and Humanities, to be serving the interests of too few in American society – in effect representing a public subsidy of private tastes and interests that should be forced to sustain themselves in the commercial marketplace (Samuelson, 1989; Jarvik, 1997). From these various neo-conservative perspectives, the post-Carnegie-I support for expanded federal aid had been a mistake, and a retrenchment to more traditional instructional purposes, if not outright elimination, was in order. It is this line of thinking that has buttressed the periodic major attempts to eliminate federal funding for public broadcasting since the passage of the public broadcasting act in 1967. There have been several such efforts, in the early 1970s, early 1980s, and mid-1990s (see Section III, D below). That critique has continued to the present day and is a regular staple of political and cultural commentary supported by the Heritage Foundation and other conservative funding agencies.

---

3 One notable exception in Denver, Colorado is at the Five Points Media Center where the co-tenants include a public television station (KBDI-TV), a community-based public radio station (KUVO-FM), and the city public access television organization (DCTV).

Finding public broadcasting under concerted attack from the left and the right, the liberal center, which during the late 1970s and early 1980s was otherwise under assault on a wide range of more general social and economic issues, felt much of its ground shifting, and the then recent consensus over the unquestioned value of steadily and substantially increasing federal support for public broadcasting began to unravel. That pattern of uncertainty has continued well into the late 1990s, and public broadcasting itself continues to be unable to articulate a clear vision of what is meant by its claim to being a public enterprise and how that unexpressed philosophy should translate into a larger and more effective role in American social experience. With a few arguable exceptions (e. g., Duggan, 1992) there remains little evidence of public broadcasting leaders (including board members, chief executives, senior managers, and producers in the various national, regional, and local station organizations) being able to write or speak at length and in depth about the philosophy, history, and social expectations of their institution, let alone the broader realm of related questions about its role in American culture, politics and social order. In short, one of the major constraints on public television is its own inarticulateness and its lack of convincing discourse about its centrality to its own society.

3.4 The constraints of funding

Several difficulties have always been associated with the funding of public broadcasting, most of them involving particular structural weaknesses among the various sources of revenue. However, by far the most serious problem about funding has been its utter inadequacy. Whatever other problems it might reflect, U.S. public broadcasting simply has not had anywhere near the amount of resources necessary for it to provide the extensive range of services that are consistent with the institution's central cultural role abroad and even with the more modest U.S. models of public telecommunications.

Public broadcasting's total revenues of $1.9 billion (see Table 1) are about 4 percent of those of American commercial broadcasting, its numbers of stations are 19 percent of those in the commercial industry, and its national program production funds were one-fifth or less of what the commercial cable television industry has been spending on programs.[4] Its per capita rate of support – the annual amount of public broadcasting revenue per citizen of the country – remains well below that of all other advanced industrial first-world nations, and its program production rate, particularly in television, is far smaller than all other public service broadcasting institutions around the world.[5]

Clearly, public broadcasting's financial situation has improved considerably over the past thirty years. That growth has led to the establishment of roughly 1,000 radio and television stations, a sophisticated satellite distribution system, two full-time national networks, and various other national and regional services, thousands of hours of original programming every year, much of it of exceptionally high quality, and a professional cadre of over 10,000 employees.

The infusion of federal funds helped strengthen the other public and private sources of support (see Table 2). However, although its total funding base in the late-1990s was some ten times that of what it was in the early 1970s (see Table 1), it must be kept in mind that such growth is measured against a tiny, almost invisible baseline and is therefore deceptively large.

The specific funding problems are all serious and can perhaps best be understood by analyzing each of the key categories of support in turn.

4 Total commercial broadcasting revenues for the years 1986–1988 grew from $29.0 to $32.7 billion (Source: Morgan Stanley & Co., Inc., *Communications Industry Datebook,* August 1988) and could be estimated at about $46.0 billion in 1997 (Source: Thom Watson, APTS). In 1996 operating commercial radio and television stations in the U.S. numbered nearly 11,500 (*Broadcasting & Cable Yearbook,* 1997); total operating noncommercial stations numbered over 2,200, but of those, roughly 800 were religious, student-run or otherwise small radio stations not supported by CPB.

5 As just one simple example, the federal government of Canada provided the Canadian Broadcasting Corporation with $918.2 million (U.S. $685.2 million) in 1995–1996. The Canadian population of 30 million was about 11 percent of that in the U.S., meaning that the Canadian federal government commitment to public broadcasting was about $24 per capita versus about $1 in the U.S. See Canadian Broadcasting Corporation Annual Report (1995–1996). Note, too, that these figures do not include the additional millions of Canadian federal dollars in other national and provincial public service telecommunications programs.

Table 1: Total Funding of U.S. Public Broadcasting (Millions of Dollars)

Fiscal Year	Federal		State & Local Tax Based		Private		Non-Federal		Total	
	Total	Percent[a]	State & Local Tax Based	Percent[a]	Private	Total	Non-Federal Percent[a]	Percent[a]	All Sources	Percent[a]
1972[b]	59.8	(25.5)	107.7	(46.0)	66.8	(28.5)	174.5	(74.5)	234.3	(100.0)
1973	55.6	(21.8)	127.3	(50.0)	71.9	(28.2)	199.2	(78.2)	254.8	(100.0)
1974	67.1	(23.1)	139.1	(47.9)	84.3	(29.0)	223.4	(76.9)	290.4	(100.0)
1975	92.3	(25.3)	156.6	(42.9)	115.9	(31.8)	272.4	(74.7)	364.8	(100.0)
1976	130.1	(30.0)	175.9	(40.6)	127.3	(29.4)	303.2	(70.0)	433.3	(100.0)
1977	135.3	(28.1)	191.3	(39.7)	155.6	(32.3)	346.8	(71.9)	482.1	(100.0)
1978	160.8	(29.1)	218.2	(39.5)	173.4	(31.4)	391.6	(70.9)	552.3	(100.0)
1979	163.2	(27.0)	245.5	(40.7)	194.7	(32.3)	440.2	(73.0)	603.5	(100.0)
1980	192.5	(27.3)	271.6	(38.5)	240.7	(34.2)	512.3	(72.7)	704.9	(100.0)
1981	193.7	(25.2)	277.5	(36.1)	297.7	(38.7)	575.2	(74.8)	768.9	(100.0)
1982	197.6	(23.4)	301.0	(35.6)	346.6	(41.0)	647.6	(76.6)	845.2	(100.0)
1983	163.7	(18.2)	318.3	(35.4)	417.1	(46.4)	735.5	(81.8)	899.2	(100.0)
1984	167.0	(17.1)	334.5	(34.3)	472.8	(48.5)	807.3	(82.9)	974.2	(100.0)
1985	179.2	(16.3)	358.4	(32.7)	558.7	(51.0)	917.1	(83.7)	1,096.3	(100.0)

Fiscal Year	Federal		Non-Federal						Total	
	Total	Percent[a]	State & Local Tax Based	Percent[a]	Private	Total	Non-Federal Percent[a]	Percent[a]	All Sources	Percent[a]
1986	185.7	(16.4)	378.8	(33.4)	569.5	(50.2)	948.3	(83.6)	1,134.0	(100.0)
1987	243.0	(18.8)	389.2	(30.1)	662.3	(51.2)	1,051.5	(81.2)	1,294.5	(100.0)
1988	247.5	(18.1)	415.9	(30.4)	704.4	(51.5)	1,120.3	(81.9)	1,367.8	(100.0)
1989	263.9	(17.0)	454.0	(29.3)	830.7	(53.6)	1,284.7	(83.0)	1,548.7	(100.0)
1990	267.4	(17.0)	473.8	(30.0)	840.2	(53.0)	1,314.1	(83.0)	1,581.5	(100.0)
1991	333.4	(19.4)	503.4	(29.3)	884.0	(51.4)	1,387.5	(80.6)	1,720.9	(100.0)
1992	373.8	(20.9)	484.5	(27.1)	931.8	(52.1)	1,416.3	(79.1)	1,790.1	(100.0)
1993	369.5	(20.6)	475.1	(26.5)	945.4	(52.8)	1,420.6	(79.4)	1,790.2	(100.0)
1994	329.9	(18.4)	509.5	(28.4)	955.1	(53.2)	1,464.7	(81.6)	1,794.6	(100.0)
1995	338.4	(17.7)	560.5	(29.2)	1,018.4	(53.1)	1,578.8	(82.4)	1,917.2	(100.0)
1996[c]	338.9	(17.3)	517.6	(26.5)	1,099.1	(56.2)	1,616.8	(82.7)	1,955.7	(100.0)

a All percentages are of total federal and non-federal income.
b First year for which detailed non-federal data is available.
c New accounting systems adopted, discouraging direct comparison of data to previous years. See Corporation for Public Broadcasting, 1997.

Source: America's Public Television Stations Corporation for Public Broadcasting.

Table 2: Federal Funding of U.S. Public Broadcasting (Millions of Dollars)

Authorizing Legislation for CPB Funding	Fiscal Year	Corporation for Public Broadcasting		Facilities		Other	Total Federal Funds
		Authorization	Appropriation	Authorization	Appropriation	Grants and Contracts	
Public Broadcasting Act of 1967 (PL 90-129)	1963–67			–	32.0		32.0
	1968	9.0	–	–			
Public Broadcasting Financing Act of 1970 (PL 91-411)	1969	9.0	5.0	12.5	3.2	8.2	
	1970	20.0	15.0	15.0	5.4	20.4	
	1971	35.0	23.0	15.0	11.0	34.0	
CPB Appropriation Authorization (PL 92-411)	1972	35.0	35.0	15.0	13.0	11.8	59.8
	1973	45.0	35.0	15.0	13.0	7.6	55.6
CPB Appropriation Authorization (PL 93-84)	1974	55.0	47.8[a]	25.0	15.7	3.6	67.1
	1975	65.0	62.0	30.0	12.0	18.3	92.3
Public Broadcasting Financing Act of 1975 (PL 94-192)	1976[b]	110.0	96.0	30.0	12.9	21.2	130.1
	1977	103.0	103.0	30.0	14.0	18.3	135.3
	1978	121.0	119.2	30.0	18.0	23.6	160.8
	1979	140.0	120.2	40.0	18.0	25.0	163.2
	1980	160.0	152.0	40.0	23.7	16.8	192.5
Public Telecommunications Financing Act of 1978 (PL 98-214)	1981	180.0	162.0	40.0	19.7[a]	10.0	193.7
	1982	200.0	172.0	20.0	18.0	7.6	197.6
	1983	220.0	137.0[a]	15.0	15.0	11.7	163.7

Authorizing Legislation for CPB Funding	Fiscal Year	Corporation for Public Broadcasting Authorization	Appropriation	Facilities Authorization	Appropriation	Other Grants and Contracts	Total Federal Funds
Omnibus Reconciliation Act of 1981 (PL 97-35) and FCC Authorization Act of 1983 (PL 99-272)	1984	145.0	137.5	12.0	11.9	17.6	167.0
	1985	153.0	150.5	–	24.0	4.7	179.2
	1986	162.0	159.5	24.0	22.9[a]	3.3	185.7
Consolidated Omnibus Budget Reconciliation Act of 1985 (PL 99-272)	1987	200.0	200.0	28.0	20.5	22.5	243.0
	1988	214.0	214.0	32.0	21.3	12.2	247.5
	1989	238.0	228.0	36.0	20.0	15.9	263.9
	1990	254.0	229.4[a]	39.0	20.0	17.9	267.3
Public Telecommunications Act of 1988 (PL 100-626)	1991	245.0 +200.0[c]	242.0[a] +56.8[c]	42.0	21.8	12.8	333.4
	1992	265.0	251.0 +76.3	42.0	22.9	23.6	373.8
	1993	285.0	253.3 +65.3	42.0	21.3	29.6	369.5
Public Telecommunications Act of 1991 (for 94-96)	1994	310.0	275.0	42.0	24.0	30.9	329.9
	1995	375.0	285.6[a, d]	29.0	23.8	338.4	
	1996	425.0	206.3[a, d]	15.5	42.1	263.9	
	1997	d	260.0[a, d]	15.25[d]	21.0		
	1998	d	250.0	d			
	1999	d	250.0	d			
	2000	d	300.0				

a Less than final appropriation due to impounding, recission, or sequestration.
b CPB data for 1976 includes transition quarter (appropriations, $17.5 million).
c Added figures are for the Satellite Replacement Fund (originally authorized at $200.0 million).
d Legislation not finished as of December 1997

Sources: America's Public Television Stations; Corporation for Public Broadcasting National Telecommunications and Information Admin.

3.4.1 Tax-based funding

Tax revenues for public television are provided at federal, state and local levels, though the latter is small and insignificant. In virtually all instances federal and state funding is appropriated from general treasury revenues. Unlike the situation abroad, and contrary to repeated recommendations of national task forces and study commissions, there are no special taxes dedicated to public broadcasting, such as license fees.

a) Federal funding
Other than the relatively small amounts of ETV facilities and ITV production support prior to the late 1960s, federal revenues were unavailable for noncommercial broadcasting. After the 1967 legislation and the creation of CPB the total amount of federal support (for CPB, facilities, and ITV) grew from some $7 million in 1966 to nearly $300 million in 1997. But by any expectation that public broadcasting should become a major influence in American life, such figures remained tiny.

Additionally, the efforts to generate the federal funds have proven constantly to be difficult and to provoke controversy. They have required the expenditure of considerable amounts of political capital and energy by public broadcasting leaders, and they have regularly been subject to serious reconsideration and even cuts. Those realities have had substantial costs that many people would consider to be too high. For such a relative pittance, public broadcasters have had to engage in constant, intensive lobbying and begging, thereby exposing themselves to regular political oversight and its vicissitudes and requiring them to divert considerable energy and resources from other presumably more essential tasks, such as program service development and production. Those efforts have likewise systematically undercut public broadcasting's independence and narrowed its own vision for itself.

When Carnegie-I first proposed a system of federal funding, it envisioned a taxing mechanism that would generate substantial and increasing revenues placed in a trust fund so that regular government influence over their disbursement and use would be prevented. It was felt that nothing like the receiving-set licensee fee so common in most other countries would be feasible. Nor was it thought appropriate that advertising revenue should be permitted. Instead, funding proposals focused on various tax options, particularly on the sales of receiving sets, on commercial broadcasting revenues or profits, and on commercial uses of the spectrum. Yet none of these had sufficient political support, and when the 1967 act was passed it left the matter of federal funding up to Congress and the president as part of the annual authorizations and appropriations process typical for the vast majority of government programs. Furthermore, the amounts generated by that process were initially quite low, well below even the modest levels that Carnegie had contemplated as necessary for a minimally effective public-service enterprise.

Within a few years the weaknesses of the annual authorization and appropriation process became widely apparent, particularly in the wake of the Nixon administration's veto of the 1973 authorization measure and associated charges of political interference with the CPB board and public affairs programming (Carnegie II, 1978, p. 205; Rowland, 1976). Many public broadcasters still held out hope for a dedicated, more permanent source of federal funds, but because the political will for establishing such a mechanism did not seem to be strong enough and because it was unclear that even a trust fund would be free of regular appropriations review by Congress, a compromise arrangement was reached. The new scheme had three essential principles: funds for CPB would come from general treasury revenues with authorizations guaranteed five years in advance and appropriations for three of those; the amount of federal funds would be generated by a "system match" formula that constituted a fixed ratio between federal funds and the total amount of nonfederal financial support (NFFS) raised by all the licensees up to the ceiling provided by the authorizations; and the amounts to be distributed to the different media (radio and television) and to the licensees would be stipulated statutorily. These provisions went into effect in 1975 and were extended and adjusted in 1978.

For a period the new provisions seemed to be having positive effects (see Tables 1 and 2). The guaranteed authorizations were progressively high enough (from $65 million in 1975 to $220 in 1983) to encourage significant NFFS growth under the system match formula, and the terms of that ratio, initially 1:22 (federal to nonfederal), were improved to 1:2. Total nonfederal income more than doubled between 1975 and 1981 ($272.4 million to $575.2 million).

However, at the very moment of its initial success the new federal funding mechanism began to break down in significant ways. The main difficulties were that the 1975 law's multi-year authorizations, which had been in effect barely two years, were reduced from five to three years in the 1978 act; the three-year advanced appropriations were actually only being made in the first of the three years, thereby making them, in effect, only two-year advances; and the authorization and appropriation steps remained separate, as with all government programs. The result was that the federal funding process was not at all long range, nor was it particularly well insulated, in that it was requiring public broadcasting to return to the administration and Congress at least every two years to seek renewed appropriations. Then, during the Reagan administration's major federal budget reassessments of 1981–1983 the actual appropriations for public broadcasting, which had reached a peak of $172 million in 1982 were rescinded and cut. Federal support for CPB fell back to $137 million in 1983, and the facilities funds, which had peaked at $23.7 million in 1980, dipped to $11.9 million in 1984.

During the mid- and late 1980s the situation improved somewhat, as the CPB appropriation rose to $229.4 million and the facilities program to $20 million by 1990. But in spite of these improvements the situation remained tenuous, the stable federal funding recommended by Carnegie-I was still out of reach. Even the more modest, but carefully crafted compromise principles for federal revenue generation in the 1975 and 1978 financing acts were in shambles. For two years (1984–1986) public broadcasting had actually been without federal authorizations, and for all intents and purposes the system match mechanism had been abandoned, as the actual federal appropriations fell well short of the amounts that would have been generated by the existing NFFS ratio. Public broadcasters struggled long and hard during the 1983–1986 period to secure renewed multi-year authorization measures. However in 1984 two such bills, seemingly well supported by Congress, were vetoed by the president, and

those vetoes were sustained. It was not until 1986 that an authorization measure was finally signed. Yet even then the advance authorizations were only for three years, until 1990, and the appropriations
only for two, until 1989. In 1988 a new authorization bill was passed,
but again for only another three years, and the eventual appropriations through 1992 continued to fall short of the authorized amounts.

Similar conditions dogged the facilities program. Although the
Reagan administration had failed to eliminate facilities support, it
succeeded in greatly reducing the authorizations for several years
and forcing the appropriations to level out at about $20 million a
year. By 1997 that figure had fallen to $15 million.

Much of the overt Reagan-era hostility to public broadcasting
funding began to ebb during the first two years of the Bush administration. Public broadcasters were also blessed during that period
with the passage of an important three-year satellite replacement
program (1991–1993). However, there was reason not to overinter-
pret those improvements. The authorizations were well below the
levels the old system match formula would generate, and the actual
appropriations continued to be less than even those authorizations
(Robertiello, 1990).[6] The facilities funds were also far below what
was necessary to build a truly substantial multichannel system of
public radio and television. Meanwhile, under the Gramm-
Rudman-Hollings deficit reduction program, those already reduced
CPB and facilities appropriations came to be subject to "sequestration" (further fixed-percentage reductions). Likewise, although the
satellite program has been treated as an additional benefit, it almost
certainly had the effect of helping to restrict the growth in both CPB
and facilities funds (Robertiello, 1990). Furthermore, the three- and
two-year authorization-appropriation process, particularly with the
annual sequestration battles, kept public broadcasting on a short
tether. Its leadership and supporters appeared to have given up hope
of any major funding increases and of anything like the long-prom-

6 Had the match system been working in the late 1980s, it would have generated $630-650
   million in federal funds for 1991 or 1992, or over twice what had been appropriated in the
   1988 law. Similarly in 1996 the match system would have generated roughly $800 million,
   or about four times what was appropriated ($206 million).

ised middle- or long-range guarantees of even the modest amounts it was receiving.

During the 1980s, public broadcasting continued to enjoy sufficient bipartisan congressional support to prevent a hostile administration from realizing its goal of eliminating federal funding. That support even permitted certain recoveries by the late 1980s. But that help proved to be too weak to prevent such assaults from regularly reappearing, particularly under the guise of the seemingly more objective criteria of budget deficit reduction targets.

Evidence of the continuing problem reappeared in the mid-1990s, when after the Republican victories in the 1994 congressional elections, new House Speaker Newt Gingrich and other leaders vowed to "zero out" federal funding for public broadcasting. As in previous such attacks, the public outcry and public broadcasting's organized opposition led Congress to retreat from the most draconian measures (Molotsky, 1997). Nonetheless CPB's previously approved higher forward funding for the late 1990s (appropriated at $312 million for 1996) was partially rescinded, dropping from $285 million in 1995 to $260 million in 1996 and to $250 million for 1998 and 1999.

In the fall of 1997 Congress agreed to a new set of increases, appropriating $300 million for CPB for fiscal year 2000, and $21 million for Public TV/Funding Program Financing (PTFP) for 1998. There even appeared to be progress toward federal funding of a public broadcasting digital transition plan, with Congress and the White House seriously considering a three-year $771 million grant (1999–2001) to help meet the total projected cost of $1.7 Billion. The latter would be in the spirit of prior moments of special federal help for periodic major public broadcasting initiatives such as the original satellite implementation and subsequent replacement projects.

Even with the renewed upward trend of federal authorizations and appropriations, plus the prospects for special major technological upgrade projects, the fact remains that the recurrent experience for public broadcasting has been one of regularly being forced back into the defensive posture of having to appeal annually for every funding measure, while also frequently having to struggle against recisions in appropriations taking place during the years for which they have been granted. Signs of the continuing tenuousness of federal funding for public broadcasting have been the several instances where annual appropriations for CPB and PTFP have had to be made without benefit of prior authorizations.

The effects of this process continue to focus public broadcasting leadership energies on short-term problems and to bind it tightly to the political agenda of the moment. As revealed during the 1990–1991 efforts to prepare for the next reauthorization bill (to extend to 1996 the legislation that would expire in 1993), and then the mid-1990s struggles against total elimination, public broadcasting has had neither the time nor the energy to stand back from these essentially annual funding struggles to look ahead and plan for any significant rearticulations of its purpose and needs. This condition also has made public broadcasting vulnerable to the temptations of undue caution and self-censorship as occasioned by expression of concerns by key congressional figures about programming topics and bias.

Altogether, then, the very mechanisms of the federal funding process, as much as the inadequate amounts, almost guarantee that public broadcasting will remain capable of only the most modest reassessment of its goals and capacities, and of being able to be as vigorously independent as desirable. It can reorganize a particular national program service office, align itself with a renewed national interest in education or prepare for a new digital transmission system, but it still cannot plan for, let alone implement, significant, far-reaching changes in the entire range of services and national and local delivery means.[7]

7 During 1990–1991, with the quality of U.S. education becoming a salient political issue, CPB and others began to re-emphasize the educational nature of public broadcasting both to justify the new authorization bill and to seek special smaller allocations in various education funding bills. Although useful in the short term, this tactic was a political expedient that was at odds with much of the general audience programming trends in public broadcasting since Carnegie-I and that in any event did not constitute a major reassessment of overall goals and services. By the late-1990s, with the federal appropriations re-improving somewhat, the educational emphasis had ebbed and elements of it were having considerable difficulty sustaining federal support (Bedford, 1997a).

b) State and local funding

As suggested in Section I, the origins of U.S. public broadcasting lie in a close association with the formal structures of education, particularly with the public school system and public universities. Those institutions are the primary province of state and local governments, not federal or national authorities, as is typically the case abroad. That tradition of decentralized educational responsibility explains much about why state and local government support for educational or public broadcasting has always been a larger source of capital and recurring revenue than federal income (see Figure 1). That support has been channeled primarily through university licensees and state educational and telecommunications authority station boards. Increased numbers of stations licensed to such institutions as well as support for various state and local instructional programs, accounted for a considerable portion of the system growth in the 1960s and 1970s. Steady increases in that form of support during the late 1970s and early 1980s, when state government budgets were otherwise widely leveling off or dropping, did much to offset the reductions in federal support. That growth has remained remarkably solid (with only a modest fall-off in 1992 and 1993) even through the breakdown of the system match principle in the federal funding process and the continuing fluctuations in congressional support through the 1990s.

However, while state and local support was significant and even increasing, the fact remained that its growth was slow and modest enough to guarantee only minor continued increases in public broadcasting facilities and program services. Proportionately it also declined from about 50 percent of overall public broadcasting revenues in the early 1970s to about 30 percent in the late 1980s and since.

State government funding also varied widely in type and amount across the country; many states did not make public broadcasting a high priority. Even where such support was substantial, it was typically annual and at the most biennial in character, its overall levels showed no dramatic increases, and its actual proportion of overall public broadcasting funding was still shrinking. Thus, while state support remained a substantial pillar of U.S. public broadcasting, it was unclear whether it could become the basis for anything more significant (that is, for a major increase in the numbers of noncommercial public-service channels and program efforts).

State funding had always been predicated on the educational and instructional potential of public broadcasting. The strength of its persistence and even growth over the years suggested the possibility of a continuing willingness of states to invest in the enterprise. It also was clear throughout the late 1980s that many state governments were intrigued by the possibilities of more sophisticated educational telecommunications, particularly under the rubric of "distance learning." As improved quality of education became a popular political response to questions about economic recovery, state governments were widely offering incentives to all levels of education (elementary and secondary schools, junior colleges and universities) to become much more involved in the use of advanced technologies to deliver instructional programs. As always before in debates about the uses of new technologies in education, the premises of such initiatives were hotly argued, but the renewed state interest in the matter suggested possibilities for continuing to develop the state commitment to the educational public broadcasting enterprise. A few people within public broadcasting had always seen the potential of expanding the linkages in this realm, particularly through the "public telecommunications center" or "public TelePlex" concepts (Central Educational Network, 1989; Hall and Fellows, 1990), but public broadcasting seemed never able to develop national programs that would explore the full service and funding potential of such models. As a result, few public broadcasters were directly and forcefully testing the states' willingness to work with them in this area and thereby leverage more state funding.

This ambiguity about the future of the relationship to formal education has remained throughout the 1990s. The rapid expansion of the Internet and World Wide Web has stimulated the search for new technology applications in all the major educational purposes – K-12, vocational training, higher education, continuing education and professional certification. There always have been competitive forces at work in the efforts to determine how best to use newer technologies to deliver formal instruction. The on-line, interactive world invites further competition for public broadcasting, from private and public interests alike. As the on-line culture grows, it is likely that such competition will increase and all the traditional institutions of educational delivery, including public broadcasting, may find that their claim on state and local funding, however limited before, will continue to be limited without a clearer redefinition around such methods and opportunities. Meanwhile in keeping with the longstanding pattern, the continuing reliance on state funding reinforces the diffuse institutional structure and national program weakness of U.S. public broadcasting.

Figure 1: Sources of funding for U.S. public broadcasting 1979 and 1995

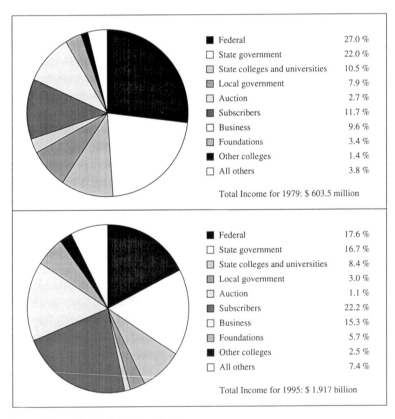

■ Federal	27.0 %	
□ State government	22.0 %	
▦ State colleges and universities	10.5 %	
▤ Local government	7.9 %	
□ Auction	2.7 %	
▨ Subscribers	11.7 %	
□ Business	9.6 %	
▦ Foundations	3.4 %	
■ Other colleges	1.4 %	
□ All others	3.8 %	

Total Income for 1979: $ 603.5 million

■ Federal	17.6 %	
□ State government	16.7 %	
▦ State colleges and universities	8.4 %	
▤ Local government	3.0 %	
□ Auction	1.1 %	
▨ Subscribers	22.2 %	
□ Business	15.3 %	
▦ Foundations	5.7 %	
■ Other colleges	2.5 %	
□ All others	7.4 %	

Total Income for 1995: $ 1.917 billion

Source: Corporation for Public Broadcasting

3.4.2 Private funding

As a matter of law and regulation, U.S. public broadcasting is officially "noncommercial." As such, although having no dedicated source of federal national funding as in the license fee mechanism abroad, it also has been restricted in its forms of nontax-based funding. Its response has been to develop several streams of revenue available to it within the U.S. world of nonprofit institutions, as for instance in the arts, culture and education. Such sources have included membership subscriptions, commercial underwriting, and foundation grants. Altogether these various forms of private funding grew at substantial rates after the early 1970s. Accounting for only about one-fifth of all public broadcasting funds in 1970, they amounted to more than a third by 1980, and then during the 1980s they more than trebled, accounting for well over half throughout the 1990s. The success of private funding was such that it came to replace state and local tax-based funds as the dominant form of public broadcasting support. Among its elements have been two principal forms that merit brief discussion.

a) Memberships and subscriptions
Up through the late 1950s, memberships and subscriptions were little used outside of a few listener-supported radio stations and the new community corporation ETV licensees. In time, particularly with the emergence of the Carnegie notion of public broadcasting, stations of all sorts began soliciting membership subscriptions, even eventually school and university licensees. Such patronage practices were already common in the arts and other cultural and social activities, as in the support of symphony orchestras, opera companies, museums, and hospitals. Their adoption in noncommercial broadcasting reflected a certain expectation that public radio and television might play comparable roles in communities around the country. By the late 1980s membership solicitation came to provide over 20 percent of public broadcasting's total income, standing at 23 percent in 1996.

The initial rapid growth and sustained availability of such support had been highly encouraging for public broadcasting throughout the

1970s. It signaled a sort of audience loyalty and commitment that offset the discouraging news of regularly low ratings. It also provided a significant margin of increased income for public stations, permitting the necessary extra element in various important program service and capital projects. Further it helped build the NFFS base and was therefore part of the original system-match federal funding logic.

But there always have been certain reservations about the role and costs of such support. For instance, it raises a fairness issue, about whether viewers and listeners should have additional responsibilities for public broadcasting above and beyond the funds they provide through taxes. Simultaneously, it raises the publicness question – that is, for whom does public broadcasting exist and by whom should it be controlled? Only about 10 percent of the regular public broadcasting audience subscribes. Consequently there has emerged the implication of a special set of rights for that group in determining program service content. Such rights often seem to be acknowledged by fundraising campaigns that impress on the audience the extent to which their contributions are necessary to confirm station decisions about purchasing or producing particular programs. Those appeals have led to questions about how much disenfranchisement of the rest of the taxpaying audience might be occurring.

Meanwhile, the considerable efforts necessary to secure subscriptions have had other substantial costs. Station managements have to invest considerable amounts of time and energy in their fundraising efforts. They have had to build up large development staffs, and in many cases, particularly in public television, they have had to make trade-offs for such activities against local program planning and production efforts. In many U.S. public television stations the local program production staffs have been eliminated or folded into the development office, so that their sole or major local production activities have become the periodic fundraising appeals. As a result much of the community program service effort has been absorbed by the local cable access groups who quite often have little or no relationship with the public broadcasting licensee. This drift has exacerbated the estrangement between public broadcasters and the independent production communities; most significantly, it has helped take public broadcasting out of the realm of local political and social affairs. Particularly in television, public broadcasting's identity has been increasingly that of an outlet for a national service, not as a forum for local voices and issues.

Finally, there has been the continuing question about the long-term prospects for membership revenue. With federal deregulation permitting increases in cable subscription fees, with the persistence of various special pay services on cable, and with the changes in the federal income tax law governing deductions of charitable contributions, it was unclear whether individual membership could be expected to grow much more.

The FCC's reluctance to maintain firm cable must-carry provisions for public television stations also seemed to undermine the subscription base. As a result public television had to expend considerable energy, and political capital, just to restore the minimum terms of traditional local reception guarantees. Those efforts diverted attention from the broader questions about the desirability and costs of this entire system of revenue generation; perhaps more important, they also diverted public broadcasters and interested political parties from working on the even larger task of framing a wider vision for the service. This situation remains a concern even after the Supreme Court, in 1997, albeit by a slim 5–6 majority, determined that the must-carry rules were constitutional (Turner Broadcasting System, Inc. v. FCC, 1997).

b) Underwriting and advertising

Industrial and corporate support for programming and even transmission operations became perhaps the most sensitive area of public broadcast funding. Never explicitly defined and authorized in legislation, the practice of soliciting underwriting developed early in the history of community ETV licensees, where appeals to foundations and various other private interests had become, like individual membership subscriptions, a symbol of its legitimacy as a particular kind of cultural institution and as a material necessity. In time, as public broadcasting's popularity grew and its evening audiences took on a particular demographic character – somewhat disproportionately upscale, professional and politically significant – many national and local corporate interests began to perceive important public relations and political value in reaching such audiences with news of their support for certain kinds of programs. At first, such identification was possible only in brief, strictly regulated underwriting credits. But these practices became increasingly liberalized as program costs rose, federal funding proved more problematic and corporate interests in reaching public broadcasting audiences grew. Over time federal policy actually began to encourage expansion of private, commercial support and even outright advertising.

All of these tendencies were reflected in the experience of the Temporary Commission on Alternative Financing (FCC, 1983) which, as part of its 1982–1983 study of the nonfederal income potential for public broadcasting, actually conducted experiments in public broadcasting advertising. Though not willing to recommend advertising's permanent emplacement, the TCAF actually helped legitimize the serious discussion of advertising's merits and at the very least fostered an environment more congenial to liberalized sponsorship. The TCAF report recommended practices that the FCC soon authorized as "enhanced underwriting," thereby taking public broadcasting a significant step further into the realm of direct commercial advertising. During the 1980s and 1990s such support grew by 65 percent, from less than 10 percent to about 16 percent of all public broadcasting revenues.

Public broadcasters and their critics have remained sharply divided over this issue. There were strong concerns that any increasing commercialization of public broadcasting was unhealthy, that it drove the institution ever closer to the programming and audience considerations that guide commercial broadcasting and against which public broadcasting must stand. At the very least, questions were asked about what programming efforts and voices went unheard when underwriting resources were unavailable. Another practical concern was that increased commercialization would seem to threaten all the other significant forms of revenue generation without any guarantee that it would offer sufficient replacement funds. Other observers, however, felt that none of the other forms of financial support would ever provide the extent of revenue necessary for public broadcasting to survive, let alone to grow and substantially increase its range of services and appeal. From this perspective the argument was that there were no realistic alternatives to increased commercial revenues and that although there were dangers associated with them, they could be managed well enough to ensure that the better, unique characteristics of public-service programming would persist and even prosper. The latter position was strongly reiterated in 1997 with the publication of a new proposal for partial, weekend commercialization of public television (Grossman, 1997).

Whatever the relative merits of these arguments, they tended to occur outside any sustained debate about the purposes and needs of public broadcasting. Even by the late 1990s there remains little recognition that the measure of increased commercialization's merits or demerits should be taken only in light of a clearer sense of public broadcasting's objectives.

4. Summary: a proposal for structural and process changes

All this evidence of the way public broadcasting works in the U.S., and careful comparisons with its counterparts abroad, suggests that what now exits is dysfunctional and actually counter to the best prospects for public service programming. In no major respect is U.S. public broadcasting working as effectively as it should. By virtue of decades of no or relatively low levels of national policy support and through a long process of resigned accommodations to that condition, public broadcasting has developed a thoroughly ingrained pattern of trained incapacity. It does some things very well, but by comparison with its counterparts abroad it is unable either to imagine or to work toward a broader role for itself in U.S. culture. Therefore, it is necessary to consider certain major structural changes.

Among those are:
– the consolidation of national-level public broadcasting organizations for programming and policy development purposes;

- a complementary consolidation of local and regional licensees;
- more centralized national programming production capacity in public television;
- a dramatic increase in the volume of programming produced by and for public television and radio at all levels;
- the reorganization of such production in full-fledged, complementary national and local multiple-program services; and
- the generation of far more resources to support those efforts.

4.1 Consolidation of national organizations

As suggested in Section II above, in other countries there tend to be only one or two national public service broadcasting organizations, e. g., the BBC and Channel Four in the UK, the ARD and ZDF systems in Germany, the ABC and SBS in Australia, the NHK in Japan or the CBC in Canada. In those instances where there are more than one organization, they typically are organized around distinctly articulated program services, and in most cases there is no division of public radio organizations.

In that light the variety of corporate structures in the U.S. tend to be wasteful and ineffective in providing the best, focused administrative structure for national public broadcasting. CPB only appears to be similar to its national counterparts abroad (BBC, CBC, NHK). Its name belies its essential lack of authority. Under current law it continues to have limited program commissioning authority and for the most part can only pass through funds to the stations and other entities. Unlike its counterparts it produces no programming, operates no networks, and owns no stations. Even its role in policy leadership is suspect, because of ambiguities in the law and the existence of a large array of other interests, many of them at the national level.

PBS has some program commissioning authority, and it does schedule the national service. But its program funding is so limited ($291.6 million in 1996) and its station governance structure so powerful, that it still tends to provide only a single national service that is much more restricted than its counterparts abroad. Even its several instructional services are merely supplementary. They do not constitute full-fledged universally available public television program streams. To this day PBS, and by extension all of public television, cannot take full advantage of its satellite and local transmission capabilities.

At the same time, PBS does not have the authority to represent public television politically. That task is assumed by a separate lobby group, America's Public Television Stations (APTS). Like PBS, APTS is a membership group that also is hamstrung by the multiplicity of its members' interests and jealousies. It has no authority or incentive to provide much long-term planning. And yet for many in the press and in the public at large, PBS is still invested with the presumption of speaking for all of public television, and, regardless of how erroneously, for all of public broadcasting.

NPR combines its operational roles in production and programming with representation. But, as with PBS, NPR finds itself competing with other formal or informal associations of licensees and program services that also lobby separately in response to competing agendas.

Meanwhile a consistent major theme of the several task forces studying U.S. public broadcasting since the mid-1960s has been a recommendation for the creation of a national program trust fund to concentrate available national program resources and planning. Such a step would eliminate much of the current overlap and redundancy among program planning and commissioning authorities. It might not, however, go quite far enough, leaving considerable program authority in the separate national and regional producing and distribution agencies.

Accordingly it might well be worth considering whether U.S. audiences would be more effectively served if, as abroad, all the various functions of major national public service broadcasters were consolidated in one federally chartered and funded organization. Such an organization could retain the CPB name, and it would likewise be possible to retain the PBS and NPR identities, perhaps as national programming divisions, as in the old NAEB model. It also would be possible to guarantee elements of licensee involvement in the new entity's governance, but the control would be limited. It would not constitute the complete ownership reflected in the current system.

The new structure also would be much more aggressive in its program production and programming roles. It would be expected to own and exploit significant production facilities, as well as commissioning authority. It also would be expected to develop a series of different, multiple-program streams in each medium, e.g., three or four in radio, two or three in television, and many others on-line. Those services would be managed separately from one another, as in the national models abroad, but they would share facilities, technical resources and representation functions (for an unfulfilled but still compelling initial model of this concept see Gunn, et al., 1980). A recent, though much belated attempt to implement part of that model is reflected in the discussions about forming PBS-2 (Brockinton, 1997).

4.2 Consolidation of local organizations

There are now over 350 local public television stations and nearly 1,800 public radio stations. Some of these are part of state networks, but overall they tend to operate independently of one another. Most notably, while they may have available to them various program sources, they tend to use those services as supplements to a single national PBS or NPR service. That is, they do not group themselves around separate national program streams as in the BBC TV 1, 2, and Radio 1, 2, 3, 4 or CBC English 1, 2 and French 1, 2 models.

This strong pattern of local presence would be highly prized if it were accompanied by significant amounts of local programming production. But in far too many cases, particularly in public television, there are only a few, i.e., less than a dozen, hours of local program production a week. In radio local production is statistically much more prevalent, but it is all too frequently limited only to large amounts of music programming. The music formats mask the dearth of local news, public affairs and information services. With few exceptions, the significant NPR news and information services are not supplemented by equally long-form and in-depth content at the local, state or regional levels.

To overcome such a lack of programming presence, it would be advantageous to consolidate stations and services in the various localities and regions. In one respect such concentration might be treated as a cost savings measure (fewer staff members and facilities), and it could readily result in elimination of many entities, leading to the survival of perhaps less than 100. But overall its justification would lie in what it would allow the licensees to do that they cannot now accomplish, as, for instance, in more clearly differentiated program services. Indeed, although the per hour or other units of cost should be lower due to administrative efficiencies, the total costs for this sort of wide ranging program effort would almost certainly be higher, as a result of the vastly increased amount of program material.

It should be emphasized that such consolidation should not occur solely for the sake of eliminating competition among local or regional entities. The purpose of this change, and the measure of its success, would be in the broadened range of complementary services occasioned by the sharing of resources and the associated synergies of creative and fiscal cross-subsidy. Duplication should be discouraged, but consolidation without significant diversity of program results would be a failure. In fact, some of the larger entities entering into such arrangements would have to approach the challenge as one of thoroughly rethinking their missions and transforming themselves into broader-ranging program service organizations, not simply as exercises in taking over and absorbing others.[8]

---

8 Tentative tendencies with regard to both national and local consolidation efforts are evidenced in recent discussions about the merger of the two major public radio program networks, National Public Radio (NPR) and Public Radio International (PRI) (Adelson, 1997), and efforts by CPB to encourage cooperative ventures and even consolidation among public television licensees in so-called "overlap markets," but as a matter of national policy or simply as a general understanding among the parties involved, it does not appear that there is an appreciation of how such initiatives will permit public broadcasting services to grow and expand.

4.3 Dramatically increased funding

The total revenues of U.S. public broadcasting are around $1.9 billion. Of that only about $300–350 million comes from the federal government. Such a figure is embarrassingly small by comparison with other major industrial nations.

The small amount of federal revenue has at least three unfortunate consequences. One, it is not large enough to sustain the volume of program production and acquisition necessary to build even a single national service of the range, volume and quality typical abroad. Two, it also makes it difficult to contemplate building a truly strong set of complementary national program services. Three, it forces public broadcasters to spend far too much time seeking other funding, principally in the form of commercial "underwriting " and individual memberships (subscribers).

Over time the underwriting system has evolved first into "enhanced underwriting," then into direct sponsorship, and now outright advertising. In the process it has seriously compromised the noncommercial nature of the public service enterprise. The effects are clear in many cities where many U.S. public television stations may be said to have already been transformed into only a slightly higher quality of independent commercial television.

But equally as insidious is the time and energy the advertising and membership activities sap from program planning and production. As a result, public broadcasting management is increasingly less about programming and more about selling and marketing.

In recent years the assault on federal funding has become so heavy that many in public broadcasting have assumed that it will be eliminated entirely, or remain at some level even more modest than that of the present. The public broadcasting response has been to despair of federal support and to all but cease working for it.

This is an unfortunate tendency at just the moment when the real prospects for generating tax-based federal dollars that could be dedicated to public broadcasting are becoming far larger than at any time in its history. The source of those revenues would be the proceeds from the auctions of new or newly freed spectrum and from taxes on the transfer (sales) of licenses. Estimates of the total value of these proceeds vary considerably. Auctions alone have accounted for about $10 billion in recent years. Together auctions and taxed sales licenses might amount to $100 billion in the next five years. If that figure was to be the target for the trust fund endowment for public broadcasting, it would yield roughly $5 billion a year, fully 15 times the current amount of federal funding. With funding at that level, public broadcasting could eliminate all of its advertising and yet still have the sums necessary to support vastly increased amounts of production and multiple-program services to be developed by the dramatically restructured and consolidated national and local public broadcasting enterprise.

Currently the spectrum auction proceeds are being used solely in federal budget deficit reduction. They have not been linked in any way to the provisions of public service to which they are technologically related. Likewise, the spectrum auction notions in recent legislative proposals are weak, inadequate versions of what is being proposed here. The bills in the 104th Congress contemplated selling only the spectrum assets of public broadcasting itself. They made no provision for the dedication to public television of the proceeds of the auction of any other portion of the spectrum. Nor did they provide for tapping the profits earned by selling assets whose value rests in their license to use publicly owned spectrum space. Some in public broadcasting did propose raising revenues for a trust fund from a mixture of auction, transfer fees and noncommercial spectrum leases (U.S. House, 1995, pp. 20–21), but the total value of the endowment sought in that proposal was only $4.0 billion, far short of the amount necessary to propel public broadcasting into a more significant role.

In this light, public broadcasting itself and those who claim to support it should be making the case for a major "public dividend" program to support the institution. That plan would articulate the details of the trust fund and the reformation of the structural elements. The public dividend plan would, however, be premised on the linkages among all three elements of reform – organizational consolidation, increased programming production and increased funding. Again, it is crucial that public broadcasting's leadership clearly and strongly articulate the extent of the vision, and fiscal expectations, outlined here. Tepid responses to the current trust fund proposals and failure to press for substantial support for it would reflect a serious shortcoming and continue the low-vision tendencies of the past two decades (for an example of this problem see Bedford, 1997b).

Conclusion

This model is only preliminary, but it suggests much about how one would be able to help U.S. public broadcasting become far more central in the nation's broadcasting and telecommunications culture. If it is not adopted, the U.S. public service institution will continue to be a political football kept under serious constraints, as merely a weak derivative of the far larger, more powerful commercial system.

Without such a bold, new vision and reorganization plan, and a significantly stepped-up investment of public support, public broadcasting also will be driven ever more thoroughly into the arms of commerce itself, losing whatever modest protections it still retains from the pressures of the marketplace. Absent a renewed social contract and a clearer set of public culture values, public broadcasting will continue to harbor a limited vision for itself. It will likely, therefore, continue to slide into a posture of reducing its audiences to consumers and abandoning its traditional commitments to them as citizens in civil discourse. As such it will never measure up to its counterparts abroad and it will continue to betray the dreams of its best supporters and thinkers at home.

Bibliography

Adelson, Andrea (1997). "Talking Stage: Public Radio's Top Voices Discuss Harmony of Merging," *The New York Times*, November 24, p. C 11.

Avery, Robert K., ed., (1993). *Public-Service Broadcasting in a Multichannel Environment*. New York: Longman/Annenberg Program in Communication Policy.

Avery, Robert K. and Robert Pepper (1980). "An Institutional History of Public Broadcasting," *Journal of Communication* 30:3 pp. 126–138. Barbieri, Richard and Jack Robertiello, (1990). "TV, Radio Face Different Revenue Picture," *Current,* July 23, 1990, p.1.

Barnouw, Erik (1966). *A History of Broadcasting in the United States, Vol. 1, A Tower in Babel*, New York: Oxford University Press.

Bedford, Karen Everhart (1997a). "CPB Hangover: Ready to Learn Double Funding," *Current*, December 1, p. 1.

Bedford, Karen Everhard (1997b). "Coonrod, Brugger: Wait and See What Happens with Spectrum Fee," *Current*, December 1, p. 7.

Blakely, Robert J. (1979). *To Serve the Public Interest: Educational Broadcasting in the United States*. Syracuse, NY: Syracuse University Press.

Blanchard, Simon and David Morley, eds., (1982). *What's This Channel Fo(u)r? An Alternative Report*. London: Comedia Publishing Group.

Blumler, Jay G. and T. J. Nossiter, eds. (1989). *Broadcasting Finance in Transition: A Comparative Handbook*. New York: Oxford University Press.

Briggs, Asa (1961). *The History of Broadcasting in the United Kingdom. v. 1. The Birth of Broadcasting, 1896–1927*. London: Oxford University Press.

Brockinton, Langdon (1997). "A double vision at PBS (Public Broadcasting System may create second network)," *Mediaweek* 7:42, November 10, 1997, p. 5.

Broadcasting. (1989). "New public TV service names board," 18 September, p. 65.

Broadcasting & Cable Yearbook (1997)."Year in Review: Broadcasting and Cable 1996," p. xxi.

Browne, Donald R. (1989). *Comparing Broadcast Systems: The Experiences of Six Industrialized Nations.* Ames, IA: Iowa State University Press.

Carnegie Commission on Educational Television (1967). *Public Television: A Program for Action* [Carnegie I]. New York: Bantam.

Carnegie Commission on the Future of Public Broadcasting (1979). *A Public Trust* [Carnegie II]. New York: Bantam.

Central Educational Network (1989). *The Public Telecommunications Complex*, (March 1989).

Commission on Freedom of the Press (1947). *A Free and Responsible Press.* [Report of the Hutchins Commission]. Chicago: University of Chicago Press.

Communications Act of 1934, PL 73-415, ch. 652, 48 Stat. 1064.

Corporation for Public Broadcasting (1997). Public Broadcasting Revenue Fiscal Year 1996. Washington, DC: CPB.

Day, James (1995). *The Vanishing Vision: The Inside Story of Public Television.* Berkeley, CA: University of California Press.

Dewey, John (1927). *The Public and Its Problems.* Fort Worth, TX: Holt.

Drickey, Janice (1989). "Larry to the Third Power," *Current*, December 11, 1989, p. 23.

Duggan, Ervin S. (1992). "The Future and Public Broadcasting," *Aspen Institute Quarterly* 4:3, pp. 14–37.

Educational Television Facilities Act of 1962. PL 87-447, 87th Congress, 2d Sess., May 1, 1962.

Engleman, Ralph (1996). *Public Radio and Television in America: A Political History.* Thousand Oaks, CA: Sage Publications.

Federal Communications Commission (1946). "Public Service Responsibility of Broadcast Licensees," 7 March 1946 [Blue Book], in Frank J. Kahn, ed., *Documents of American Broadcasting,* 4th ed. Englewood Cliffs, N.J.: Prentice Hall, 1984, pp. 148–163.

Federal Communications Commission (1952). "Sixth Report and

Order." 17 Reg. 3905, 3908 (41 FCC 148, 158), April 14, 1952, in Kahn, pp. 182–190.

Federal Communications Commission (1983). "Final Report," Temporary Commission on Alternative Financing for Public Telecommunications.

Federal Communications Commission (1987). Report No. MM-263 Mass Media Action on Fairness Doctrine, August 4, 1987.

Fox, William John (1997). "Junk News: Can Public Broadcasters Break the Tabloid Tendencies of Market Driven Journalism? A Canadian Experience," Discussion Paper D-26, Joan Shorenstein Center on the Press, Politics and Public Policy, John F. Kennedy School of Government, Harvard University.

Frost, S. E., Jr. (1937). *Education's Own Stations: The History of Broadcast Licenses Issued to Educational Institutions*, Chicago: University of Chicago Press.

Grossman, Lawrence K. (1997). "Introducing PTV Weekend" Available from *Current Online* at http://www.current.org/weekend/wklg597.html.

Gunn, Hartford N., Jr., et al. (1980). "In Search of the Formula: The System Planning Project Papers," *Public Telecommunications Review*, 8:3 (May/June) pp. 7–102.

Hall, George and James Fellows (1990). "TelePlex: A Brave New World, a Bold New Concept," *Current*, June 4, p. 39; see also the regular columns in *Current* by George Hall on behalf of the PBS Office of New Technology Initiatives (ONTI), 1988–1989.

Hoffman-Riem, Wolfgang (1996). *Regulating Media: The Licensing and Supervision of Broadcasting in Six Countries*. New York: Guilford Press.

Horowitz, David (1995). *Public Broadcasting and the Public Trust*. Los Angeles, CA: Center for the Study of Popular Culture.

Horwitz, Robert Britt (1989). *The Irony of Regulatory Reform: The Deregulation of American Telecommunications*. New York: Oxford University Press.

Jarvik, Laurence A. (1997). *PBS, Behind the Screen*. Rocklin, CA: Forum.

Jones, Stephen B. and Willard D. Rowland, Jr. (1990). *NET Programming: A History and Appreciation of the Programming Serv-*

ice of National Educational Television, 1952–1970. Contract No. A86-31, Library of Congress, February 1990.

Ledbetter, James (1997). *Made Possible By ... The Death of Public Broadcasting in the United States.* New York: Routledge, Chapman & Hall.

Lewis, Peter M. and Jerry Booth (1990). *The Invisible Medium: Public, Commercial and Community Radio.* Washington, DC: Howard University Press.

Lippmann, Walter (1922). *Public Opinion.* Orlando, FL: Harcourt Brace Jovanovich.

McChesney, Robert W. (1993). *Telecommunications, Mass Media, and Democracy: The Battle for the Control of U.S. Broadcasting, 1928–1935.* New York: Oxford University Press.

Molotsky, Irvin (1997). "How One Tough Bird Survived the Attack on Public Broadcasting," *The New York Times*, November 11, p. B1.

Nerone, John C., ed. (1995). *Last Rights: Revisiting Four Theories of the Press*, Urbana: University of Illinois Press.

Peterson, Theodore (1956). "The Social Responsibility Theory," pp. 73–103 in Fred Siebert, Theodore Peterson and Wilbur Schramm, eds., *Four Theories of the Press.* Urbana: University of Illinois Press.

Public Broadcasting Act of 1967, PL 90-129, 81 Stat. 365 (7 November 1967).

Public Telecommunications Financing Act (1978), PL 95-567, 92 Stat. 2405 (2 November, 1978).

Public Telecommunications Act of 1988, PL 100-626, 102 Stat. 3207, 7 November 1988.

Radio Act of 1912, PL 62-264, ch. 287, 37 Stat. 302.

Radio Act of 1927, PL 69-632, ch. 169, 44 Stat. 1162.

Robertiello, Jack (1990). "CPB Spending Set for 1993," *Current*, (6 November 1990), p. 1.

Rowland, Willard D., Jr. (1976). "Public Involvement: The Anatomy of a Myth" pp. 120–126 in Douglass Cater and Michael J. Nyhan, eds., *The Future of Public Broadcasting.* New York: Praeger.

Rowland, Willard D., Jr. (1993). "Public-Service Broadcasting in the United States: Its Mandate, Institutions and Conflicts," in Robert K. Avery, ed., *Public-Service Broadcasting in a Multi-channel Environment.* New York: Longman/Annenberg Program in Communication Policy.

Rowland, Willard D., Jr. and Michael Tracey (1990). "Worldwide Challenges to Public Service Broadcasting," *Journal of Communication* 40:2 , pp. 8–27.

Rowland, Willard D., Jr. and Michael Tracey (1991). "The Case for Public Television: Its Principles, Purposes and Promise," A Report Commissioned by America's Public Television Stations, Washington, D.C., February, 1991.

Samuelson, Robert J. (1989). "Highbrow Pork Barrel," *Newsweek,* 21 August 1989, p. 44.

Schwartz, Bernard (1973). *Economic Regulation of Business and Industry,* Vol. I. New York: Chelsea House.

Somerset-Ward, Richard (1993). "Public Television: The Ballpark's Changing." Background Paper in *Quality Time?: The Report of the Twentieth Century Fund Task Force on Public Television.* New York: Twentieth Century Fund Press.

Telecommunications Act of 1996. PL 104-104, S. 652, February 8, 1996.

Turner Broadcasting System, Inc. v. FCC (1997), U.S., No. 95-992, March 31, 1997.

Twentieth Century Fund (1993). *Quality Time?: The Report of the Twentieth Century Fund Task Force on Public Television.* New York: Twentieth Century Fund Press.

U.S. House (1995). "The Future of Public Broadcasting: Hearing Before the Subcommittee on Telecommunications and Finance of the Committee on Commerce, House of Representatives," 104–37, September 12, 1995.

U.S. Post Office Department (1914). "Government ownership of electrical means of communication" Letter from the postmaster general, in response to a Senate resolution of January 12, 1914. 63d Congress., 2d Sess. Senate. Doc. 399, U.S. G. P. O.

White, Llewellyn (1947). *The American Radio.* Chicago: University of Chicago Press.

Funding and Economics of American Public Television

James Ledbetter

Contents

1. Introduction 74
   1.1 A brief history of the medium 74
2. The Corporation for Public Broadcasting 75
3. Programming funds 76
   3.1 How much is spent on programming? 77
   3.2 Cost of production 80
4. Alternative services 82
5. Cultivation of private funds 83
6. Convergence of public and private broadcasting 87
7. New media and the future 90
8. Conclusion 92
Bibliography 92

1. Introduction

The funding system for American public television (and public radio as well), particularly in comparison to its international counterparts, is unique in its complexity and variability. Although the current system of American public television was designed in the late 1960s with federal and state funds as its primary means of support, today private funds – including viewer contributions and corporate sponsorship – dominate public television programming and, to a lesser degree, public television operations. This paper provides an explanation of how American public television has historically been funded, its current financial makeup, and the implications that current trends and developments in new media are likely to have on the funding of American public television in the future.

1.1 A brief history of the medium

Especially when compared to older and more-established public television systems – such as the British Broadcasting Corporation (BBC) – American public television is highly decentralized. Instead of functioning as a centralized network, American public television is actually an amalgamation of approximately 350 individual stations, each with its own broadcasting license, individually tailored broadcast schedule, and station management. This structure is a holdover from the era prior to the 1967 Public Broadcasting Act, the federal legislation that first created the modern system of recurring, federal taxpayer support for public radio and television.

In the 1950s and 1960s, what is today called public television was an even looser amalgamation of educational television stations,[1] supported primarily by state legislatures, universities, and foun-

---

1 The Carnegie Commission is generally credited with coining and popularizing the phrase "public television"; its report, entitled *Public Television: A Program for Action*, was released in early 1967, and formed the blueprint for the federal legislation enacted in November of the year.

dation grants (most significantly, the Ford Foundation, which provided more than $200 million for public television and radio programming and facilities in the 1950s and 1960s).[2] The first federally funded television programming came under the auspices of the 1958 National Defense Education Act, a section of which was earmarked for "research and experimentation in the new media," for which it budgeted a total appropriation of $18 million.[3] Congress passed the Public Broadcasting Act in 1967 with an initial annual Congressional appropriation of $5 million. In 1996, the Congressional appropriation for public television and radio was $250 million; the appropriation that President Clinton signed into law in late 1997 allowed for $300 million annually in fiscal year 1999.

2. The Corporation for Public Broadcasting

The Corporation for Public Broadcasting (CPB) is the closest American approximation to a centralized public television agency, in that CPB receives funds primarily from the federal government and is governed by a presidentially selected board of directors.[4] Although President Johnson – whose administration authored and passed the Public Broadcasting Act – promised that public broadcasting would one day be funded through a steady, renewable mechanism – for example, an excise tax on televisions, or a television license fee comparable to the BBC's – neither his administration nor any subsequent administration or Congress has ever developed one. Instead,

---

2 For details, see Marilyn A. Lashner, "The Role of Foundations in Public Broadcasting, Part II: The Ford Foundation," *Journal of Broadcasting*, vol. 21, no. 2 (Spring 1977), pp. 235–54 and *Ford Foundation Activities in Noncommercial Broadcasting 1951–1976* (New York: Ford Foundation, 1980).

3 W. Wayne Alford, *NAEB History Volume 2: 1954 to 1965* (Washington, DC: National Association of Educational Broadcasters, 1966), p. 53.

4 The CPB is not, however, an agency of the federal government. It is a private, not-for-profit corporation. As such, it is not subject to certain laws that govern federal agencies, such as the Freedom of Information Act.

the CPB has historically been dependent on one-, two-, or three-year Congressional appropriations.

As of 1997, total income and expenditures for American public broadcasting now approaches $2 billion annually (for means of comparison, that figure is more than triple what it was in 1978). Broken down into component sources, this funding came from the following sources, in decreasing order of magnitude:

Subscribers:	22.2 %
State government:	16.7 %
Business:	15.3 %
Federal government (CPB):	14.9 %
Public universities:	8.4 %
Federal government:	7.0 %
Grants and contracts Foundations:	5.7 %
Local government:	3.0 %
Private universities:	1.4 %
Other public colleges:	1.1 %
Auction participants:	1.1 %
All other sources:	7.4 %[5]

By statute, the CPB may not spend more than 5 percent of federal allocations on administration and overhead expenses; CPB also spends a roughly comparable amount on "system support."[6]

3. Programming funds

A fundamental shift in the method of funding public broadcasting occurred in 1974. During the presidency of Richard Nixon, public television came under ferocious attack: in part because its adminis-

---

5 These figures are contained in *Frequently Asked Questions About Public Broadcasting 1997* (Washington, DC: Corporation for Public Broadcasting), p. 7.

6 Ibid, p. 8. In fiscal year 1997, for example, 6 percent of the CPB budget, or $13.0 million, was spent on "system support."

trators and on-screen talent were deemed to be politically "liberal" and opposed to the Vietnam War, and in part because the Nixon White House orchestrated a media campaign against the high salaries paid to two public television commentators. The Nixon administration wanted at times to eliminate the entire system of federal funding for public broadcasting, and came close to achieving this goal; overwhelming Congressional support for the medium kept it alive.

As a fallback measure, the Nixon administration tried to eliminate public affairs programming from public television, and used its appointments to the CPB's board of directors to funnel more money to the local stations thought to be more politically conservative. In large part responding to this decentralization pressure from the Nixon White House, the public broadcasting system moved the bulk of its programming funding away from large, Washington-centered organizations – such as CPB and PBS – and toward the individual stations themselves. Thus in 1972 stations received about 12 percent of CPB funds in the form of Community Service Grants (CSGs), while the national entities CPB and the Public Broadcasting Service (PBS) received a combined total of 76 percent of national funding for program production in distribution. Today, that structure is reversed: for fiscal year 1997, the total budget for CPB was $260 million, of which approximately $170.7 million – or 65.65 percent – went directly to affiliated stations in CSGs (Radio CSGs $40.5 million, TV CSGs $130.2 million) and $60.7 million – or 23.3 percent – in "programming support" ($17.3 million for radio programming, and $43.4 million for television programming).[7]

3.1 How much is spent on programming?

It is difficult to find a precise figure for how much public television spends on programming per year. As noted above, CPB spends $43.4 million on public television programming. Clearly, however,

---

7 These figures come from *Frequently Asked Questions About Public Broadcasting 1997* (Washington, DC: Corporation for Public Broadcasting, 1997), p. 8.

since CPB directly funds only a tiny portion of the offerings on public television, the true figure for programming expenditures is many times higher. The 1996 PBS annual report notes that the "1,936 hours of first-run programs distributed by PBS's National Program Service in Fiscal 1996" cost an estimated $291.6 million.

The overall, systemwide funding of public television programming, however, is much larger than these amounts would indicate. This is because a large percentage of programming distributed through PBS is paid for not by the central organizations of PBS or CPB, but by the public television stations themselves. The programming burden is not shared equally among stations: although there are more than 350 television stations nationwide affiliated with PBS, the overwhelming majority of them produce no programming that is distributed throughout the system. Instead, a handful of large stations throughout the system – such as WGBH (Boston), WETA (Washington, DC), WNET (New York/New Jersey), KCET (Los Angeles) – provide a majority of hours that are distributed nationally.

One station alone, for example, WGBH, is responsible for the regular systemwide distribution of such PBS staples as *The American Experience, Frontline, Mobil Masterpiece Theatre, Mystery!, NOVA,* and *This Old House,* as well as several others. This indicates a system tilted in favor of the stations. As one marketing businessman who specializes in selling public television time to underwriters put it: "There are a few things producers have to realize about the process by which public television does business. The individual station is where the real authority lies ... though three stations in particular wield far more power than the others: WGBH, WNET in New York, and WETA in Washington. PBS itself controls nothing. PBS does present itself as a purchaser of programming, and it is an important one. But that is because Congress funds it through the Corporation for Public Broadcasting. That money is disbursed by PBS to the stations, which, in turn, return some of that money to PBS to act as one source of acquired programming."[8]

8 Keith Thompson, president Public Broadcast Marketing, quoted in "Babes in adland," by Neal Winstock, *TV World*, September 1994. p. 13.

To get a clearer picture, then, of how much money the public television system spends on program production, one must go beyond the programming figures offered by PBS and CPB and look at the expenditures of the stations themselves. The top ten stations (measured by how many hours of programming they provide to the national system),[9] have a collective budget of approximately $489 million. Of that, their collective programming budget is just below $300 million.[10]

That figure, however, only takes into consideration the programming that is distributed nationwide through PBS. What the viewer sees on public television at any given moment may well come from a number of different sources: it may be locally produced by the station; it may have been produced by an independent ousted operator (such as the Children's Television Workshop); it may come from an outside underwriter (such as General Electric, which offers *The McLaughlin Group* to public television stations for free); or it may have been purchased from a program service other than PBS (see below).

In 1991, the CPB hired the Boston Consulting Group (BCG) to study, among other things, the complex funding of public television.[11] Using figures from 1989, the BCG determined that member stations spent $467 million on program production and acquisition.[12] Even using conservative estimates, the overall programming budgets for public television's 352 stations today is almost certainly between $800 million and $1 billion – which rivals the programming budget for the commercial networks.

9 According to *Quality Time? The Report of the Twentieth Century Task Force on the Future of Public Television* (1992) the stations are: KCET-Los Angeles; KQED-San Francisco; WMPT-Maryland; WBGH-Boston; KTCA/KTCI-St. Paul; KCPT-Kansas City; WNET-New York; WHYY-Philadelphia; WQED-Pittsburgh; and WETA-Washington, DC.

10 These figures are derived from adding the television programming and production figures in each of the ten stations' annual reports. In each case, the most recently available statistics were used of August 1997; depending on the station, those may be 1996, fiscal year 1996, or 1997 figures.

11 The final product was released as *Strategies for Public Television in a Mullet-channel Environment* (Washington, DC: Corporation for Public Broadcasting, 1991).

12 Ibid, "PTV Costs and Revenues by Function," p. 7.

3.2 Cost of production

The cost to produce programming for American television can vary greatly, depending on region, type of programming, and the degree of private sponsorship. Historically, American public television has created little to no original dramatic or comedy series (a notable exception was The Adams Chronicles, produced in the mid-1970s to coincide with the celebration of bicentennial of the Declaration of American Independence).

There are several reasons for that surprising shortcoming. One is that in 1967, when federal funding for American public television began, American commercial networks produced a glut of drama and comedy series. Since public television was founded as an alternative to those networks, it concentrated its meager resources on areas where commercial television was deemed to be lacking educational programming, public affairs, and cultural offerings such as opera and ballet.

A second reason is financial. Unlike the American commercial networks (ABC, CBS, NBC, and the Fox network), neither CPB nor PBS operates a national production company. All American public television programming must therefore be acquired from either a local station or an independent production company. Since the British Broadcasting Corporation (BBC) spends so much more on television production than any public entity in the United States, and because its programs require no translating or dubbing to be intelligible to an American audience, most of the best known drama series on American public television have been produced or co-produced by the BBC. Former PBS president Larry Grossman once quipped, "I can't imagine where American public television would be if the British didn't speak English."

American public television's heavy reliance on foreign producers effectively displaces domestic providers. Labor unions operating in the television business – which includes writers, directors, and many different technical unions – have tried to press this point with public television executives for decades. The unions regard the PBS-BBC alliance as an avoidance of their clout in broadcasting, one that saps American jobs.

Both original programming produced for American public television – including documentaries such as *The Civil War* and regular series such as *Washington Week in Review* – and programming acquired from abroad are almost always paid for by private underwriters. Initially, corporate underwriters were attracted to public television because it was dramatically cheaper to sponsor. Former Mobil vice president for public affairs Herb Schmertz has written that when WGBH first contacted him about underwriting *The Forsyte Saga* in the early 1970s, he had never watched any of it, but he was attracted by the prospect of being able to purchase 39 hours of television at the price of $390,000 (or $10,000 per hour).

More recently, however the costs of public television production have increased, to the point where they often exceed those of some commercial productions. In 1994, for example, CPB and PBS spent $1.5 million to develop 22 episodes of a game show called *Think Twice,* even though only four episodes were ever distributed on the PBS national schedule. In the mid-1990s, public television talk show host Charlie Rose stopped using the facilities of New York's WNET to produce his nightly talk show because they were prohibitively expensive; he was able to get a more reasonable deal from the private Bloomberg information network. Public television documentaries funded through Boston's WGBH are budgeted at between $500,00 and $1,000,000 an hour as opposed to $150,000 on cable channels such as the Arts & Entertainment network.

High production costs from an obvious constraint on the type of programs that the system can produce, and create a system that, in many instances allows underwriters essentially to dictate what will and will not be shown. Local programming, despite being one of the original mandates of American public television, is prohibitively expensive to most of the public television system, because corporate underwriters would prefer to associate their products and services with national programming for maximum promotional effect. Public television is so dependent on underwriters to meet its production costs that programming appears on public television even when public television administrators would prefer not to broadcast it. In one instance, Mobil's Schmertz has said that "the entire public television establishment was opposed to" acquiring the British drama Upstairs,

Downstairs when it first became available, but Mobil was "just as adamantly in favor of it." Schmertz's position was: "If you're not going to acquire it, we're going to acquire it anyway, and find some way to run it on American television whether it's commercial or public." PBS gave in.

Without such contemporary enthusiasm, however, American public television is often powerless to fulfill its mission. In 1985, Barry Chase, PBS vice-president of news and public affairs, said bluntly: "We'd love to do a program on the history and role of business in America. But who will underwrite that?"

4. Alternative services

While most lay viewers do not distinguish between PBS, their local station, and an entity called "public television," it is important to remember that PBS is merely one distributor among many in the American public television universe (albeit the largest and one of the oldest). Another such service is the Minnesota-based Independent Television Service (ITVS), which is the result of a legislative mandate. As Congress debated the 1988 reauthorization of public broadcasting's appropriation and authorization, it determined that the system was excessively dominated by a small number of producers and stations, and created a separate system designed for "independent" producers i. e., those outside the normal channels of PBS and its largest stations. ITVS was slated to receive $6 million annually for three years.[13] While ITVS was slow to get its initial projects on the air, today it funds some of the most innovative and challenging material on public television, including the acclaimed human rights series *Rights & Wrongs* and *The Gate of Heavenly Peace*, a stunning documentary about Tiananmen Square.

Another public television service that now reaches most PBS-affiliated stations is the Boston-based American Program Service

13 James Day, *The Vanishing Vision* (Berkeley: University of California Press, 1995), p. 324.

(APS), founded in 1980 as part of a regional educational broadcasting service. Unlike PBS, APS is not a membership organization; rather, stations purchase material from APS on a program-by-program basis. The Summer 1997 APS catalogue offers hundreds of hours of programming to public television stations. The bulk of this material – including documentaries, crafts, how-to and children's programming – is provided for free to local stations. Program costs are picked up by local underwriters and by toll free merchandise offers linked to the programs. Nearly all of public television's 350 stations pick up some programming from this exchange.[14] APS did not receive any money from the CPB in 1996; it is, however, listed in CPB literature as a "principal source of programming" for public television.[15] APS, which operates as a nonprofit, had a reported $11.14 million in sales in fiscal year 1994.[16]

5. Cultivation of private funds

Since the early 1980s, public broadcasting has fundamentally reoriented itself: moving from a nonprofit, noncommercial educational model toward a model that actively seeks nongovernmental (especially non-Federal) sources of revenue. To a great extent this shift can be traced to 1981. The Reagan administration, for both policy and economic reasons, declined to approve increases in CPB appropriations, and in fact demanded – through a veto – that the levels be cut.[17] As a consequence, the enabling legislation for public broadcasting that Congress passed in 1981 explicitly directed public broadcasting licensees "to seek and develop new sources of non-Federal revenues, which will be necessary for the long-term support of the sys-

14 Many APS programs are among public television's best-known, including *Monty Python's Flying Circus* and *The Three Tenors*.
15 *Frequently Asked Questions About Public Broadcasting,* op cit, p. 4.
16 This figure comes from Dun & Bradstreet; APS, a division of the Eastern Education Network, is assigned the Dun & Bradstreet number 04-940-8271.
17 This shift is discussed in John Witherspoon and Roselle Kovitz, *The History of Public Broadcasting* (Washington, DC: Current, 1978), pp. 55 ff.

tem as Federal funding is reduced."[18] At the same time, Congress created the Temporary Commission on Alternative Financing (TCAF), which allowed ten public television stations to experiment with "limited advertising," and explored a variety of non-Federal funding methods, including increased individual contributions, facilities leasing, teleconferencing services, commercial use of satellite facilities, and even a national lottery.[19]

Not all of these methods have proven viable. Nonetheless, by 1995, the national system of public television was amassing $89,552 million annually in "excludable" or "entrepreneurial income"[20] – a funding source equivalent to more than one-third of the CPB Congressional appropriation which had not existed at all 15 years before.

A second important shift in public television financing that occurred during the 1980s involves the liberalization of standards for "underwriting." Even during the introduction of educational television in the 1950s, there was some degree of financing and program sponsorship from private companies.[21] Nonetheless, through the 1970s, private companies were restricted to "tombstone" announcements of their underwriting, consisting solely of the name of the company in plain type and a voice-over announcement. The TCAF encouraged public television to experiment with "enhanced underwriting" credits which were a step closer to commercial television's advertisements. In 1984, the Federal Communications Commission approved a new, liberalized set of underwriting guidelines that allowed for the use of corporate logos and moving images. Not surprisingly, this move profoundly affected companies' desire to use public television as part of their marketing strategies, and thus the

---

18 Public Broadcasting Amendments Act of 1981, H.R. Rep. No. 97–82, 97th Congress, 1st session, p. 7.

19 *The History of Public Broadcasting*, op cit, pp. 55–6.

20 *Public Broadcasting Revenue Fiscal Year 1995* (Washington, DC: Corporation for Public Broadcasting, 1996), p. 3. The comparable figure for public radio was $15.27 million. The range of items for which income is "excluded" illustrates the creative ways in which public television entities are augmenting their budgets, including – (1) production and taping (2) telecast and teleconferencing (3) studio, equipment and tower rentals (4) sales of program rights (5) public performances (6) sales and rentals of transcripts and records (7) profit subsidiaries and nonprofit subsidiaries and (8) licensing fees and revenues.

21 Examples are offered in chapter 2 of my book *Made Possible By ...: The Death of Public Broadcasting in the United States* (New York: Verso, 1997).

amount of money public television receives from corporate underwriting. In 1977, public television took in $38 million in corporate underwriting revenues; by 1995, that figure had more than quintupled, to $215,442,000.[22]

Moreover, corporate underwriters now recognize that public television expenditures are genuine marketing expenses: according to two CPB officials, a noticeable shift in funding patterns took place in the late 1980s as private funders stopped giving to public broadcasting out of their charity/philanthropic arms; instead the "donations" to public television came out of the companies' advertising and marketing divisions.[23] Not surprisingly, then, underwriters seeking to get the maximum message for their expense have leaned on PBS and individual stations to provide them with cutting-edge identification spots that more and more resemble commercial television spots. Today, the distinction between advertising and "enhanced underwriting" is practically moot. Most of the largest PBS affiliate stations already allow 30-second underwriting messages (including WNET-New York, KCET-Los Angeles, KQED-San Francisco, WTVS-Detroit and KRMA-Denver).[24] At KETC in St. Louis, nearly half of the station's entire underwriting income comes from 30-second spots. Keith Thompson, president of Public Broadcast Marketing, estimated in early 1997 that 80 percent of the U.S. population could be reached through 30-second spots on public television. In mid-1997, fourteen large public television stations reportedly signed letters of intent with an underwriting spot sales company which plannplanned to sell local "corporate support announcements" much like ads.[25]

22 The 1977 figure comes from *A Public Trust: The Landmark Report of the Carnegie Commission on the Future of Public Broadcasting* (New York: Bantam Books, 1979), p. 104; the 1995 figure from *Public Broadcasting Revenue Fiscal Year 1995* (Washington, DC: Corporation for Public Broadcasting, 1996), p. 5.

23 This observation was made by Jeannie Bunton and S. Young Lee, both of the CPB, in an interview with the author, August 1996.

24 Karen Everheart Bedford, "The Question of Length Is Really Settled," *Current*, February 17, 1997.

25 "Williams starts up rep firm to sell 'CSAs' for local stations," *Current*, July 21, 1997, p. 12. According to this article, some stations charge cost-per-thousand-viewer rates that are competitive with commercial television, while others are able to charge "three or four times" the commercial rate by emphasizing public television's uniqueness and, ironically, its lack on-air clutter.

Although currently PBS does not accept 30-second spots accompanying programs in its national schedule, it is facing increased pressure – even from public television producers – to do so. Even without accepting advertising spots, PBS now actively encourages national corporate sponsors to coordinate spots with programs. In 1996, PBS made a coordinated pitch to advertisers, reportedly offering season-long sponsorship spots on *Barney* for between $250,000 and $1.2 million.[26] In 1997, a consortium of the major producing stations (WNET, WGBH, KCET, and WETA) banded together into the PBS Sponsorship Group, which toured the country to meet with advertising executives, offering custom-designed packages in which advertisers could purchase time on a variety of PBS programs. "Welcome to the new PBS," WNET president Bill Baker told the ad executives. "Corporate messages on PBS get more creative every year. You can show products. You can use slogans."[27]

Increasing, PBS is branching off into business ventures that are less and less associated with programming. In response to Congressional pressure, PBS is relying more heavily on merchandising and licensing arrangements, its internal projections seek to bring in $5.2 million annually through licensing by the year 2000. PBS has sought to ensure that shoppers need not leave their homes to purchase PBS-related merchandise, by establishing an on-line shopping service web site. In 1997, PBS officials announced that they were consulting with Creative Artists Agency, one of Hollywood's largest and most powerful talent agencies, to establish a music label. PBS officials said in 1991 that they have contracted with a book publishing arm called PBS Books, and have announced that the organization will be pitching its programs to airlines through a service called PBS Aloft. The expansion of public television into commercial, nonbroadcasting activities is not limited to national organizations. In Grand Rapids, Michigan, for example, station WGVU offers the use of its studio and satellite uplink in return for a donation, a service called "Business Television."

26 "PBS puts more efforts into selling itself: it sets goal of boosting corporate sponsorship money by $25 million annually by 2000," *Broadcasting & Cable*, August 5, 1995.
27 "Tour aims to correct ad world's notions about PBS," *Current*, May 12, 1997, p. 1.

Perhaps inevitably in this environment, a public discussion has begun to create a full-blown commercial PBS service. In the fall of 1996, former PBS president Lawrence Grossman announced his proposal, developed with a grant from the Markle Foundation, for a two-nights-a-week commercially supported network. In Grossman's proposal, the second channel, tentatively called P-2, would supplement PBS broadcasts on Friday and Saturday nights (when PBS currently feeds no mandated programs to its affiliates).[28] P-2 would be capitalized and part-owned by large corporations (in all likelihood, related companies from the telecommunication's industry) and by affiliated public TV stations. It would charge $10 to $15 per thousand viewers in the 25–54 age range for 30-second spots; Grossman has estimated that this would require a minimum of seven minutes per hour of advertising, thus guaranteeing the commercial interruption of programs.

There is no certainty that the Grossman scheme will come to fruition.[29] But even without it, CPB has estimated that more aggressive underwriting will bring an additional $35.6 million annually into public television coffers by the year 2000.[30]

6. Convergence of public and private broadcasting

In the first decade or so of its existence, public television was to a large extent a self-contained entity. Stations did business with the CPB, PBS, National Educational Television, and regional networks,

28 The details of Grossman's proposal are cited in "Two-night commercial net discussed for public TV," *Current*, November 25, 1996.

29 Not long after the Grossman proposal was made public, officials of the Federal Communications Commission rejected the idea of creating a commercial public television service. Nonetheless, the Grossman proposal represents only a more explicit version of the commercialism that already dominates public television. Some version of what Grossman envisions is almost certain to come to light in the 21st century.

30 This figure comes from the Lehman Brothers analysis assembled for CPB in 1995 and released as *Common Sense for the Future* (Washington, DC: Corporation for Public Broadcasting, 1995), p. 9. Lehman Brothers also projected that aggressive underwriting could bring in an additional $29.1 million for public radio.

and tended to keep their distance from the rest of America's commercial media. That relationship has changed dramatically. Both PBS and individual public television stations have begun to converge with the American and international media business, so much so that public television has begun to look like a marketing arm for commercial media companies. Indeed, there are virtually no major media conglomerates that lack some form of strategic business partnership with public television.

This multimillion dollar embrace of commercial media has not come about by accident: it is purposeful, deliberate policy made by public television's leaders. When Ervin Duggan took over the presidency of of PBS in February 1994, he announced 16 initiatives he intended to accomplish in his first 120 days; these were known collectively as "Operation Momentum."[31] Operation Momentum included a number of multimillion dollar strategic partnerships, including:

– An agreement between PBS and Turner Home Entertainment to market and distribute PBS Home Video. The terms of this deal included an agreement from Turner to match PBS's investment in new programming dollar for dollar for new titles to be aired on PBS and marketed under the PBS Home Video label. Thus Turner – now a division of media giant Time Warner – is seeding its own video distribution business by helping to create programs on public television.

– PBS, KCTS (Seattle), and Buena Vista Television unveiled a joint venture to bring *Bill Nye, The Science Guy* to public television. During weekday afternoons, the program runs on public television stations; on weekends, it runs on commercial television stations, courtesy of Buena Vista, which is a division of Disney-Capital Cities-ABC.

– To produce *PBS Mathline*, PBS secured a $3.2 million grant from the CTIA Foundation, and $2 million from AT&T, one of the world's largest telecommunication's companies; US West also announced in 1995 that it was hooking up with CPB for a similar

---

31 *Taking Stock: A Report on the 'Conversation' Among PBS Member Stations*, PBS booklet, May 25, 1994, p. 6.

project. The existence of such alliances is largely kept secret from viewers, the vast majority of whom are no doubt unaware that supposedly noncommercial programming is being developed and distributed by commercial media firms. This takes the degree of private, corporate influence and input a step beyond underwriting – where a private company agrees to sponsor previously produced programs – and makes the companies more like executive producers, by picking up all or most of the production costs. One of PBS's best-known successes of the 1990s, Ken Burns's *The Civil War*, was primarily paid for by General Motors.[32] Such developments blur the lines between what are public television entities and what are commercial media entities. The best example of this confusion is the *The NewsHour with Jim Lehrer*, the star of PBS's public affairs programs. The program is produced by the Washington, DC-based MacNeil/Lehrer Productions, which in late 1994 sold two-thirds of itself to Liberty Media Corp., which is a subsidiary of TCI, the country's largest cable provider.

Increasingly, the convergence of private broadcasting interests is affecting the content of public television as well as its financing. In November 1995, PBS announced a partnership with the private media firm Readers Digest Association to produce 20 nature documentaries called *Living Edens*, a five year deal expected to infuse some $75 million into the PBS program budget.[33] The program broker and developer Devilier Donegan Enterprises, which is owned by Disney/Capital Cities/ABC, is coproducing with PBS on a three-part science series called Coming of Age, to be aired in 1998; all told, Devillier Donegan is scheduled to produce some $50 million worth of programming.[34] To date, public television administrators do not appear to be distributed about any affects that such convergence will have on their ability to serve the public-interests.

32 "When Agencies and Clients Produce the TV Programs," *New York Times*, July 8, 1991, p. D6.
33 "First series debuts with 'Digest' backing," Current, July 7, 1997, p. 1
34 "PBS announces project with Devilher, Kratts," *Current*, July 7, 1997, p.6.

7. New media and the future

One of the great weaknesses of American public television in the 1980s and 1990s has been the system's failure to adjust to the explosion of cable television. By all indications, the public broadcasting system is bound to make the same error regarding telecommunication's and new media. In 1978, a second Carnegie Commission analogous to the one that created the current system of public broadcasting issued a report calling for a systematic overhaul, including changing the Corporation for Public Broadcasting to a Public Telecommunications Trust. That advice went unheeded. Twenty years later, in its proposed fiscal year 1997 budget, the CPB has slotted a minuscule $50,000 for "support of new media" in a budget of $260 million.[35]

By contrast, public television managers have demonstrated greater enthusiasm for converting to a digital broadcasting capability. In 1996, the Federal Communications Commission (FCC) approved a plan for all American television broadcasters – commercial and public – to convert to digital broadcasting by the year 2003. Digital compression of the spectrum holds great promise for public television broadcasters: it could help resolve programming limitations through the ability to offer different programming formats simultaneously. At the same time, however, as of late 1997, it appeared that individual stations would have to bear the cost of digital conversion themselves, depending on the station, that cost was estimated at between $5 and $10 million per station, prohibitively expensive for virtually every station. Estimating the systemwide cost at $1.7 billion – and that figure is probably conservative – the CPB requested $771 million from Congress in October, 1997 to help defray the cost.[36] Since that amount represents more than double the annual federal appropriation for public broadcasting, initial Congressional reaction was understandably cool.

---

35 FY 1997 Proposed Operating Budget (Washington, DC: CPB, 1996), p. 8.
36 See *Washington Post*, October 16, 1997, p. B9.

The Congressional reaction to the digital conversion request illustrates that both the amount and direction of public television's budgets are subjected to forces well beyond the control of CPB managers. Principally, the most powerful and most volatile force has been the U.S. Congress. The Republican House and Senate victories of November 1994 created great political impetus for "zeroing out" the federal legislative support for public broadcasting. The most sophisticated form of this proposal was legislation offered by Republican Jack Fields, who proposed the creation of a public broadcasting trust fund of $1 billion.[37] Variations of this proposal have been submitted throughout the public broadcasting world, and have gathered a reasonable amount of support; as of December 1997, however, there was little consensus about the size of the fund, the sources of its original capital, and the effects that such a fund would have on public broadcasting's tax-exempt status and its ability to raise funds in other areas.

Other proposals for a renewable source of income that would be less subject to Congressional viability include a system whereby taxpayers could voluntarily donate a portion of their tax to the public broadcasting system while filling out their income tax forms (comparable to the current system of funding presidential elections). A proposal that has substantial support among academics and progressive critics of public broadcasting is to tax the advertising industry, and set aside those proceeds to fund American public broadcasting.[38] Assuming that advertising expenses on American television and radio remain the same or increase, a tax of 1 or 2 percent would replace or surpass the amount currently appropriated by Congress. As of December 1997, however, such a proposal has little support among public broadcasting administrators, and would inevitably face fierce opposition from commercial broadcasters.

37 Fields issued his legislation, "The Public Broadcasting Self- Sufficiency Act," in 1996; it did not pass that Congress.
38 The advertising tax is discussed in Edwin Baker's *Advertising and a Democratic Press* (Princeton: Princeton University Press, 1994). as well as in the final chapter of my *Made Possible By: The Death of Public Broadcasting in the United States* (New York: Verso, 1997).

8. Conclusion

Almost certainly, the convergence and commercialization of the system described in this chapter will continue to grow. The increasing use of private media corporations to fund and create programming on public television raises the question of whether the public television of the 21st century will be "public" in any way more than name only, or whether it will use the notion of public broadcasting as a method of marketing essentially commercial programming.

Bibliography

A Public Trust: The Report of the Carnegie Commission on the Future of Public Broadcasting. New York: Bantam Books, 1979.

Alford, W. Wayne. *NAEB History, Volume 2: 1954 to 1965.* Washington D.C.: National Association of Educational Broadcasters, 1966.

Avery, Robert K. and Robert M. Pepper. *The Politics of Interconnection: A History of Public Television at the National Level.* Washington D.C.: National Association of Educational Broadcasters. 1979 (Also appeared in J/F and S/O 1976 issues of *Public Telecommunications Review*).

Baker, C. Edwin. Advertising and a Democratic Press. Princeton: Princeton University Press, 1994.

Blakely, Robert J. *To Serve the Public-Interest: Educational Broadcasting in the United States.* Syracuse: Syracuse University Press, 1979.

Bleifuss, Joel. "Public Television On the Block," *In These Times,* July 8, 1996. pp. 12–13.

Brennan, Timothy. "Masterpiece Theater and the Uses of Tradition," in *American Media and Mass Culture Left Perspectives*, ed. Donald Lazere. Berkeley: University of California Press, 1987. Originally published in *Social Text*, no. 12 (Fall 1985).

Brown, Les. *TeleviSion. The Business Behind the Box.* New York: Harcourt Brace Jovanovich, 1971.

Burke, John. "Public Broadcasting Act of 1967. Part III: Congressional Action and Final Passage," *Educational Broadcasting Review.* Volume 6, number 4 (June 1972). pp. 251–266.

Cater, Douglass, "The Politics of Public Television," *Columbia Journalism Review.* July/August, 1972. 8–15.

Day, James. The Vanishing Vision. Berkeley: University of California Press, 1995.

Engleman, Ralph. *Public Radio and Television in America.* Thousand Oaks, CA: Sage Publications, 1996.

Ermann, M. David. "The Operative Goals of Corporate Philanthropy: Contributions to the Public Broadcasting Service, 1972–1976." *Social Problems* 25: 504–514.

Hoynes, William. *Public Television for Sale, Media, the Market & the Public Sphere.* Westview, 1994.

Jarvik, Laurence. PBS: Behind The Screen. Rocklin, CA Prima Publishing, 1996.

Keilner, Douglas. *Television and the Crisis of Democracy.* Boulder: Westview Press, 1990.

Lashley, Marilyn. Public Television. Panacea. Pork Barrel, or Public Trust? Greenwood Press, 1992. 147 pp.

Lashner, Marilyn A. "The Role of Foundations in Public Broadcasting Part 1: Development and Trends" *Journal of Broadcasting.* 20:4 (Fall). 529–47. "Part II: The Ford Foundation." *Journal of Broadcasting.* 21: 2 (Spring). 235–54.

Ledbetter, James. *Made Possible By.: The Death of Public Broadcasting in the United States.* New York: Verso, 1997.

McChesney, Robert W. *Telecommunications, Mass Media, & Democracy: The Battle for the Control of U.S. Broadcasting.* 1928–1935. New York: Oxford University Press, 1993.

Pepper, Robert M. *The Formation of the Public Broadcasting Service.* New York: Arno Press, 1979.

Powell, Walter W. Friedkin, Rebecca Jo. "Politics and Programs: Organizational Factors in Public Television Decisionmaking," in *Nonprofit Enterprise in the Arts. Studies in Mission and Constraint.* New York: Oxford University Press, 1986.

Powledge, Fred. *Public Television: A Question of Survival.* New York: American Civil Liberties Union. February 1972.

Public Television: A Program for Action. Report of the Carnegie Commission on Educational Television. New York: Bantam, 1967.

Public Television "Prime Time": Public Affairs Programming, Political Diversity, and the Conservative Critique of Public Television, by David Croteau, William Hoynes, and Kevin Carragee (unpublished, 1993).

Quality Time? The Report of the Twentieth Century Fund Task Force on Public Television. New York: Twentieth Century Fund, 1993.

Rowland, Willard D., Jr. "Continuing crisis in public broadcasting: A history of disenfranchisement." *Journal of Broadcasting and Electronic Media.* 30: 3 (Summer): 251–74.

Schnertz, Herb (with William Novak). *Good-bye to the Low Profile: The Art of Creative Confrontation.* Boston: Little, Brown, and Company, 1986.

Stone, David M. *Nixon and The Politics of Public Broadcasting.* Washington D.C.: Current, 1987. 85 pp.

Witherspoon, John and Roselle Kovitz. *The History of Public Broadcasting.* Washington D.C.: Current, 1987, 85 pp.

American Public Television: Programs – Now, and in the Future

Richard Somerset-Ward

Contents

1. Public television programming – today 96
   1.1 Quantification and categories 97
   1.2 Comparison to commercial television
       and cable television 98
   1.3 "Public-interest" programming 98
   1.4 Contributions to education 100
   1.5 Contribution to political process 101
   1.6 Internal production 102
   1.7 Other sources of programming 103
   1.8 Quality of programs 104
   1.9 Impact on journalistic standards 105
2. Programming for the digital future 106
   2.1 A public telecommunications alliance 108
   2.2 Nonbroadcast services 109
Bibliography 112

There are very few valid comparisons to be made between American public television and noncommercial networks in other countries. The American system is based on localism – 347 separate stations, individually licensed, having very varied purposes (some of them are specifically educational institutions, some are community stations, some are part of state-wide networks). There is very little central direction or intent. Most European and Asian systems, by contrast, are specifically designed to be national in their scope and centralized in their direction.

Public television came into being in the United States as an afterthought – it was grafted on to a flourishing commercial system whose purpose was to make money. In Europe, and in some other countries where public television came first, the full spectrum of programming was always part of the remit of noncommercial broadcasters. It was not even an option in America, where public television never had the resources or the opportunity to compete for the more expensive and profitable areas of programming that commercial stations had already colonized – amongst them, sports, feature films, comedy, and fully-equipped news services.

The earliest noncommercial stations in America, long before the system was codified as "public broadcasting" in 1967, were educational stations, pure and simple. To this day, public television is sometimes referred to as "educational television," and that remains its most powerful contribution. But it is much more, and it is the thesis of this chapter that, in the digital age, it could become *a great deal more*, if it seizes its opportunities.

1. Public television programming – today

An enormous amount of programming is available to the 347 local stations. There *is* such a thing as local programming, but few stations are equipped (or can afford) to do much of it. So they rely very largely on packaged feeds from central sources, and on programming they buy in from individual suppliers, both within and without the system. The best known of these feeds is the National Program Service (NPS) which is supplied by PBS, the stations' membership organization in Alexandria, Virginia. NPS provides the stations with their basic primetime schedule, and daytime children's programs as well.

1.1 Quantification and categories

In 1996, PBS distributed over 25,000 hours of programming to the stations, of which only 7.5 percent was accounted for by the National Program Service.[1]

– American Program Service (APS), which is an additional and alternative source of programming for the stations, currently lists 250 titles (mainly multi-part series) in its syndication service, a further 350 titles in its exchange service, and rights to about 100 specials and special series in its premium service.

The National Instructional Satellite Service feeds 1,400 hours of K-12 programming to stations, for use in schools.

– The most recent figures available for purely local production are those issued by the Corporation for Public Broadcasting for Fiscal Year 1994.[2] Of the 197 licensees surveyed, the *average* amount of locally produced programming, per station per year, was 154 hours, broken down into 135 hours of "general production," 15 hours of K-12 programming, and 4 hours of post-secondary production.

– These are the principal sources of programming, but there are many other additional sources, including (for instance) the Program Resource Group (PRG) for stations overlapped by larger stations in the same market, the Lark Group (a production and acquisition cooperative created by stations in Seattle, Houston, St. Louis, and Detroit), the Central Educational Network (CEN), and the Independent Television Service (ITVS).

1 *Americans Like What They See*: PBS Annual Report, 1996, p.12.
2 *CPB Research Notes* (No. 88, April 1996), p. 12.

– The main categories of programming are education (both formal and informal), children's programs (especially pre-school), public affairs, documentaries of all kinds, science and nature programming, and cultural affairs. American public television has no news service of its own, and no central production facility (both PBS and APS are acquirers and distributors of programming, not producers). National production is concentrated in a very few major stations.

1.2 Comparison to commercial television and cable television

Public television programming is narrower than that of the commercial networks – no sports, no comedy, very few feature films (and generally only "golden oldies"), no news bulletins, a scarcity of drama, no game shows, very few daytime talk shows. On the other hand, it is more broadly based than the cable channels, most of which are concentrated in individual "niches." To the extent that public television is also a niche broadcaster, it inhabits a variety of different niches – children's programming, science, arts and music, public affairs, etc.

Many of public television's traditional niches have been occupied by cable channels – Nickelodeon for children, The Learning Channel for education, Discovery for documentaries, Bravo and Ovation for the arts, and so on. The most obvious "competitor" to public television is Arts & Entertainment, which combines popular documentaries (e.g. the successful nightly *Biography* series) with PBS-type drama, and tactical use of high quality former network series (*Law and Order,* etc.).

1.3 "Public-interest" programming

The 1996 Telecommunications Act envisioned, but did not spell out, the idea of broadcasters having to accept "public-interest obligations." It was left to the FCC to create the necessary rules and regulations, with the Clinton Administration urging it to do so as quickly as possible – the President himself wrote an unprecedented letter to the FCC asking it to make rules to strengthen the educational programming requirement. In October 1997, under the patronage of Vice-President Gore, an Advisory Committee on Public-Interest Obligations of Digital Television Broadcasters was convened to report by June, 1998 (it immediately requested a four month extension).

"Public-interest" in broadcasting is currently defined by a small group of objectives which have been placed at the top of the agenda by politicians and pressure groups. They include the principle that all television stations, commercial and noncommercial, should include in their weekly schedules not less than three hours of "quality educational programming for children." All the usual arguments apply – is *Mr. Magoo* "quality educational programming"? Other objectives include free airtime for political candidates, the use of closed captioning for the handicapped, the adoption of an on-screen ratings system (to forewarn of violence, nudity, bad language, etc.), the regulation (or even banning) of liquor advertisements, and the use of Public Service Announcements.

Some of these objectives have, to some degree, been put into effect voluntarily, although free airtime (which is the principal objective of the politicians) is not readily available. Public television has no problem with any of them. It is, by far, the biggest supplier of quality educational programming for children (to the extent that several commercial broadcasters are prepared to pay public television to supply their own quotas of such programming), and it has no objection to free airtime for candidates, if such a system can be worked out.

If the immediate agendas of the politicians and pressure groups are ignored, then most public television programming can fairly be labeled "public-interest." This is an important point, because the commercial broadcasters, who want to have very little to do with public broadcasting (and they certainly don't want to finance it in any way) nevertheless rely implicitly on public broadcasting to provide a stable and continuing supply of public-interest programming. When American children's programming is held up as "amongst the best in the world," it is public television's programs that are being referred to. When regular and thoughtful public affairs programming is lauded, it is the nightly one-hour *NewsHour* that is most often given as an example.

1.4 Contributions to education

Public television's specifically educational programming is huge in quantity, and generally high in quality.

Its pre-school programming (*Sesame Street, Barney, Mr. Rogers' Neighborhood,* etc.) is acclaimed throughout the world and is accessible to parents and children either on PBS broadcasts or through the *Ready to Learn* service, which includes local outreach.

Public television is the largest supplier of K-12 instructional programming for schools, although it has recently suffered inroads from commercial suppliers, many of whose products are more closely tailored to the needs of teachers in classrooms (8 – 15 minute modules).

– Its adult learning services include a vast array of telecourses leading to diplomas or degrees. The *Ready to Earn* banner encompasses services that prepare students for the world of work, and adults to overcome illiteracy (*Literacy Link*) and to gain high school diplomas. *Going The Distance* enables students to earn degrees through college telecourses. More than two-thirds of America's 3,000 colleges use PBS adult learning services.

– *The Business Channel* provides more than 1,000 hours of video-based training (including desktop video-on-demand) and video conferences to more than 2,000 businesses.

– More than 1,000 hospitals use PBS' video conferencing facilities and training programs to update their staff on medical issues and techniques.

– *PBS Mathline* and *PBS Teacher Connex* supply teachers with information and courses, as well as with directions for obtaining other video and on-line services.

– The *Annenberg/CPB Channel and Web Service* provides programming and curriculum courses for educators and communities through a free satellite signal and Internet web sites. Its concentration is on math and science teaching.

1.5 Contribution to political process

Public television's national programming includes both weekly and nightly affairs shows (*The NewsHour with Jim Lehrer, Washington Week in Review, Frontline, etc.*).

Many stations also produce their own local programs, ranging from 17 stations which have their own nightly news and public affairs shows, to the production of weekly local-issue talk shows by most stations. Documentaries and occasional specials are produced at the local level, as are occasional town meetings, "meet the mayor" programs, etc. Community and state-run stations almost always play an active part in local democracy.

Election and campaign coverage on public television is more thoughtful and more issue-oriented than it is on commercial television (which is dominated by political advertising, often of a sharp and provocative nature). PBS has established *The Democracy Project* as the flagship of its political programming, both during elections and between them. It produces documentary series, interview programs, and election coverage, strictly balanced between issues and viewpoints.

For several decades, political broadcasting in the United States was based on the so-called "Fairness Doctrine." It required broadcasters to devote reasonable amounts of time to the discussion of controversial issues of public importance, and to do so fairly by affording airtime to opposing viewpoints. The Fairness Doctrine was swept aside in the 1980s, first by the courts, then by the refusal of the Reagan Administration to accept a bill reimposing the doctrine.

Absent the Fairness Doctrine, the Clinton Administration is hoping to place "public-interest" obligations on broadcasters. These might include the provision of free airtime for political candidates as a *quid pro quo* for the broadcasters having been given (for free) their new digital frequencies. The problem is that the *quo* is being demanded after the *quid* has been given.

1.6 Internal production

PBS and the American Program Service (APS) are the principal suppliers programming for public television. Neither is a producer. They acquire and they commission (often in co-production agreements with independent or foreign producers).

A great deal of public television (maybe a third) is purchased from foreign broadcasters or producers. Some of this is "reformatted" to look like American-produced programming (new narration, etc.), some of it (like the *Masterpiece Theatre* dramas) is left intact, but prefaced by an "introduction."

The principal producers of national programming are a group of four or five stations, all of them on the East coast with the exception of KCET, Los Angeles. WNET in New York, WGBH in Boston, and WETA in Washington D.C. are responsible for about two-thirds of all national production. Some of this is original production (most of the public affairs programming, for instance), but a great deal of prime-time programming is independent or foreign production syphoned through an individual station, which acts as the originator for the entire nationwide system – and takes the consequential risks (in funding or co-funding the programs).

The actual making of programs falls mostly to the independent sector – not many stations carry production staffs for national programming, and even then they are normally support staff rather than actual program-makers. Whether they are independents commissioned by individual stations (or by PBS, APS, or one of the central or regional suppliers), or they are organizations of independents formally supported by the system (like the ITVS group), they are the backbone of public television and they make the vast majority of all its programming, with the exception of local programming. The biggest of them, the Children's Television Workshop, produces almost 15 percent of all national programming.

Among the producing stations, there are pockets of expertise and experience – WGBH in Boston, for instance, is responsible for some of the most valued series – *NOVA* (science), *The American Experience* (history), and *Frontline* (public affairs documentaries) are three of the most important. WETA in Washington, D.C., has a particular expertise in news and public affairs programming (*The NewsHour with Jim Lehrer*, etc.). *The Nightly Business Review* is produced by WPBT in Miami.

Among local stations, the record is spotty. Only 17 stations produce their own nightly news show.[3] Many of the educational stations concentrate on telecourse and teaching material, and most of the state networks are heavily involved in statewide activities (many of them carry coverage of their state legislatures and other events).

So far as program costs are concerned, they are dramatically lower than commercial network costs, but very often higher than cable costs. A program for A&E's nightly *Biography* series is budgeted at $130,000 – the average for *The American Experience* on public television would be several times higher. That is partly a reflection of quality, partly of the higher audience available to public television, and partly of the availability of corporate underwriting for public television programming (in addition to contributions from PBS, CPB, and occasionally the NEA and/or the NEH, as well as foundations).

1.7 Other sources of programming

Since public television is a commissioner of programs, much more than it is an actual producer, independent American production is included within Internal Production (above). Certainly, it is true that public televison has its own independent community securely attached to it, and largely dependent on it.

The main source of outside production is, therefore, foreign production. PBS statistics show that this source accounts for about 14 percent of the NPS prime-time schedule.[4] That figure is suspect because it does not include a wide variety of programs that appear in the schedule as part of "continuing series" – e. g. BBC *Horizon* programs renarrated as part of *NOVA*, productions of the BBC Nat-

3 *Current* (October 20, 1997), p. 9.
4 *Quality Time? The Report of the Twentieth Century Fund Task Force on Public Television* (The Twentieth Century Fund Press, New York, 1993), p. 138.

ural History Unit which are similarly included in *Nature*, etc. The actual figure may be between 25 percent and 30 percent.

British programming forms the major part of this percentage, but there are also Australian and Irish productions, with a sprinkling of European programs in subtitled or dubbed versions.

Educational programming is almost entirely produced in America – much of it by independent producers specializing in the genre.

1.8 Quality of programs

A perception of quality – high quality – is generally attached to public television programming. It is seen in the respect accorded it by reviewers, and in the way most viewers distinguish it from the rest of television programming available to them. A Roper Starch tracking study for PBS[5] showed that the adjectives most often used to describe public television were "educational," "interesting" and "informative." Widely, but less often, used were "generally good," "important," "imaginative," "stimulating".

A 1996 Total Research Corporation survey[6] gave PBS less comforting news. Asked which channel respondents associated most directly with certain types of programming, the survey showed that niche cable channels – such as The History Channel, The Travel Channel, Nickelodeon, Bravo, Arts & Entertainment, The Home and Garden Channel, and others – had made small, but distinct, inroads on public television's perception as being the preeminent supplier of these programs.

---

5 Quoted by Robert Ottenhoff, Chief Operating Officer of PBS, in *Television Industry Scan* (February 1, 1997), an internal PBS document, p. 12.
6 Ibid. p. 13.

1.9 Impact on journalistic standards

American public television came into its own as a journalistic medium at the time of the Watergate hearings in 1973/74. Following hard on a blatant and fierce attempt by the Nixon Administration to stifle its independent reporting, public television not only carried the hearings gavel to gavel, but distinguished itself by the depth and fairness of its reporting and comment.

The nightly MacNeil/Lehrer programs, which had their origins in those anxious days, and which eventually developed into *The NewsHour,* established journalistic standards that quickly won the respect of politicians, commentators, and viewers. The refusal to surrender to the 20-second "sound bite" philosophy, and the determination to give ample space to the hearing of both sides of controversial issues, has made *The NewsHour* a model of what television can do, and what public television must do.

The other regular program to impact journalistic standards is *Frontline,* whose fearless, and often brilliant, in-depth reporting of important issues has won it many prizes, and the respect of both television and newspaper journalists.

In one important field, public television missed out. It was ideally suited to be the vehicle for what is now C-SPAN – the cable network which relays live (and "live on tape") coverage of Congressional proceedings and committee hearings, as well as important events from all over the nation (speeches, press conferences, etc.). This is an information service many rely upon, especially the opinion-formers, but it was a service PBS decided against supplying in the late 1970s[7], leaving the option available to a consortium of cable operators who supply the service without cost.

What all this amounts to is a very large and impressive supply of programming that is primarily educational and informational in intent. The prime-time National Program Service supplied by PBS,

---

7 The PBS System Planning Project, 1978/79, consisted of a series of project papers issued by Hartford N. Gunn, Jr., then the Vice Chairman of PBS. Project Paper No.10 (Dated May 23, 1979) recommended that PBS should develop and launch a channel which would do more or less what C-SPAN does today.

which is what most Americans recognize as "public television," is short on entertainment values and somewhat aged. It includes many fine series – *Frontline* (investigative journalism and public affairs documentaries), *The American Experience* (history), *NOVA* (science), *Nature* (natural history), *Masterpiece Theatre* (British drama), *Great Performances* (music and the performing arts), and *The NewsHour* - but all these series have been in the schedule a long time, some of them for more than a quarter of a century. Refreshment is badly needed; it requires an injection of new money and an equal injection of new imagination. The occasional fine series that come from independent producers (Ken Burns, for instance, from *The Civil War* to the upcoming *Jazz* series) do not compensate for the old-fashioned feel of the schedule – and that is a problem. The same might be said of instructional programming for the classroom (still much the same as it was in the 1970s and 1980s). Only in its children's programming has public television continuously been on the cutting edge of both popularity and educational thinking.

Nevertheless, there is a launchpad here. Public television is embedded in the consciousness of Americans. For all its clumsy structure and perennial shortage of funds, it has the makings of an organization that can flourish in the digital age. It is already a $1.5 billion industry. It has a brand image (PBS's) that is recognized nationwide. It has a wonderfully efficient satellite delivery system. And it has this vast network of local stations from coast to coast. What it needs, and what it is about to get, is a digital revolution.

2. Programming for the digital future

Already, the principal tool for this revolution has been supplied. Every television station in the United States, be it commercial or noncommercial, has been given (for free) an additional frequency on which to begin digital broadcasting in parallel with its existing analogue service. Every station is required to be broadcasting in digital format by 2003 at latest; analog frequencies will have to be returned to the government by 2006 (there may well be some slippage on this latter date if digital television sets have not been sold to at least 85 percent of households by that time; a study by Forrester Research of Cambridge, MA, in November 1997 reported that local broadcasters expect 19 percent of their viewers to have made the switch by 2001[8]).

The government's principal objective in giving stations these frequencies is to promote High Definition Television (HDTV), but nowhere is it written that stations *must* broadcast in HDTV, now or in the future. All that is certain is that they must get digital services on the air within five years (and many of them will be doing so within a few months). So, whether or not HDTV takes off, we can anticipate a great deal of Standard Definition Television (SDTV), which is also digital, though inferior to HDTV, but which has the great advantage that it uses only a small part of the digital frequency allocated to each station. Multiplexing will therefore become commonplace – the transmission of several (maybe as many as a dozen) different signals on the same frequency. For commercial stations, this is an opportunity for greater profit; for public stations, it is an opportunity – finally – to realize their mission.

Crystal ball gazing is a dangerous activity in these days of leapfrogging new technologies, but it seems fairly safe to predict that the broadcast firmament of the next ten years will include a slowly increasing amount of HDTV programming (particularly in prime-time and sports time, picking up speed as and when consumers start buying new sets in real numbers), and a great deal of SDTV multiplexing. All this will have to take place in the context of the most dramatic development now on the drawing board, which is the convergence of the TV and the PC (itself made possible by digital transmission). What it all means is that *now* is the time to be developing new services – multiple services – to make proper use of the new capacity.

---

8 Reported in *Broadcasting & Cable*, November 17, 1997, p. 10.

2.1 A public telecommunications alliance

The possibility American public broadcasters are presently considering is the creation of a large-scale alliance of users of public telecommunications, both nationally and (in literally hundreds of mirror images) locally. Such an alliance would include state and local governments, museums, libraries, civic institutions, public health networks, schools, colleges, distance learning providers, the not-for-profit community, businesses, and homes – and public broadcasters, too, for they, with their ability to distribute high speed voice, data, and video over any distance, large or small, have the potential to be the hubs of such an alliance.

On paper, it looks rather a far-fetched vision, a good talking point. But I think it is a practical possibility – because all the potential players have a need for it. All of them are under pressure to make use of the new technologies. What they lack (but what public broadcasters have) is a distribution system. Yes, it's true that they all have access to the Internet, but that is a clumsy, indiscreet, and often unreliable carrier compared to the high speed, direct, and exclusive distribution that can be obtained through public broadcasters' digital frequencies. Cable operators will be able to provide the same sort of service, but they reach less than 70 percent of homes – moreover, they will need to make handsome profits. Public broadcasters' twin strengths – a national satellite distribution system, and a local presence in practically every significant community in America – give them a considerable advantage, as does their ability to provide services at cost (or, let's be realistic, slightly above), but without having to make substantial profits.

What this posits is a public broadcasting service with two distinct roles. Broadcasting will remain the most important mission, along with the production and distribution of an increasing amount of non-broadcast programming. But public broadcasting will also become a digital services provider on a considerable scale, both locally and nationally. It has the means to do this – but does it have the will? At this moment, following the effective, but discreet, leadership of the Corporation for Public Broadcasting (CPB), it is considering the option.

2.3 Nonbroadcast services

A surprising amount of public television programming is not designed for broadcast "over the air." Schools and colleges with receiving dishes take instructional programs directly from the satellite.
*PBS On-Line, PBS Electronic Field Trips, PBS Mathline, PBS
Teachers Connex, the CPB/Annenberg Satellite Channel* are all examples of valued services for students and teachers which have no
broadcast function (though some of them certainly could have). *PBS
Plus* and *PBS Select* (which will shortly include *PBS Classics*) are
syndicated services used by stations to augment their schedules. *The
Adult Learning Service* includes such services as *Ready to Earn* (of
which *Going The Distance* is a part, giving students the opportunity
to gain a degree through college credit telecourses) and *LiteracyLink*
(which uses video, on-line, and computer technology to help adults
receive literacy instruction and gain high school diplomas). *The
Business Channel* provides businesses and other organizations with
teleconferencing and desktop video on demand. All these are examples of non-broadcast services already in place and expanding year
by year.

The new digital capacity will enable PBS and other providers to
increase both the number and the effectiveness of these services.
The new "push" technologies (data and video streaming to the desktop) are already in demand, and will become a potent tool during the
next few years. As television and computer technologies converge,
so will the requirement for distribution of digital signals – and it
won't always be by the Internet, which is a crowded and very public
carrier, unregulated, and somewhat unreliable. Indeed, one of the
services already being pioneered in Utah and Virginia is the use of
public television stations as "safe" (and very high speed) access
routes to selected web sites – thus reassuring anxious parents about
what their children may, or may not, see on the Internet.

And this is just the tip of the iceberg, because if public broadcasters (radio and television) are truly to become the hubs of telecommunications networks, then they will have to become digital services providers to a great many institutions and organizations they have
not previously worked with. Some of them (libraries and museums)

they have often thought of as competitors, but now the concept of an "electronic public library" can become a reality, and the combined resources of libraries, museums, and public broadcasting can make it a powerful tool for learning and information. The concept of an "electronic republic" (articulated by Larry Grossman, a former President of PBS, in the 1997 Webb Lecture[9]) is another viable idea – the proposition that telecommunications technology can be used to meld the United States' traditional form of representative republic with new elements of electronic direct democracy. Some would argue that it is a dangerous concept, bordering on anarchy if it is totally unregulated, but it is nevertheless something that has to be experimented with.

These are some of the more glamorous examples of digital services provision – the ones that will be debated in newspaper editorials and legislative forums – but there are many more of the "bread and butter" variety. State and local governments, for instance, forced to accept new and burdensome duties previously performed by the federal government (administration of funds for welfare, transportation, and other largescale budgetary items) are going to require high-speed and confidential transmission of information by data, voice, and graphic means. Public health networks need to inform their users, update their administrators, doctors, and nurses, and educate the population as a whole in methods of disease prevention and healthy living. In all these areas (and they are only examples) effective public telecommunications is a vital resource. Public broadcasters may be surprised to find they are the key to it – and no one can force them to become a part of it – but it is a fact that their contribution to the sort of public telecommunications alliance envisaged for the next century will be pivotal, both for them and for the other participants.

There is another good reason why this should be so. Public broadcasting needs to earn its living. Ever since its conception, it has relied on a form of public begging that is both demeaning and unpopular. "Pledge weeks" have become so deeply embedded in the

---

9 Lawrence K. Grossman, Webb Lecture, the National Academy of Public Administrators, Washington, D.C., November 14, 1997.

world of public television that few station managers or senior officials can envisage a situation in which they will be able to escape from the awful thrice-yearly penance. The gross amount raised in this way by stations in 1997 was in excess of $300 million – but no one has ever, or will ever, tell us what the *net* figure is. When you take away the cost of the studios (which some stations use only for pledge programs) and the staff and the extra programming costs, what is the actual value?

Participation as the hub of a grand public telecommunications alliance might very well enable public television to foreswear its mendicant status. As a provider of digital services, it will be earning revenues – not huge ones, but sufficient, in all probability, to pay for its expanded role as a broadcaster and program-maker – and it is quite possible that stations which choose to play an active and constructive role in the alliance, as digital services providers as well as broadcasters, will be able to abandon "pledging" altogether in a few years.

The last significant revolution in American broadcasting – the coming of cable – was blithely ignored by public television, to its great cost. Its refusal to react in any way – neither by making use of the so-called PEG channels (the public, educational, and government cable channels provided for by the 1984 Cable Act), nor by adapting and developing its own programs and schedules in the face of cable's concentration on niche programming – doomed it to what was, at best, a stand-still during years in which other broadcasters and narrowcasters thrived.

A repetition of that mistake would certainly be disastrous, possibly fatal. The more reason, therefore, to face the digital future with imagination. The technology and the means are at hand. Is the will there, too?

Bibliography

The essential documents on American public broadcasting are the reports of the two Carnegie Commissions (1967 and 1979) and the report of the Twentieth Century Fund Task Force (1993):

Public Television – A Program for Action: The Report and Recommendations of the Carnegie Commission on Educational Television (Harper & Row, New York, 1967).

A Public Trust: The Report of the Carnegie Commission on the Future of Public Broadcasting (Bantam Books, New York, 1979).

Quality Time? The Report of the Twentieth Century Fund Task Force on Public Television, with Background Paper by Richard Somerset-Ward (The Twentieth Century Fund Press, New York, 1993).

Two other publications contain much useful information:

John Witherspoon and Roselle Kovitz, edited by J.J. Yore and Richard Barbieri, *The History of Public Broadcasting* (*Current*, Washington, D.C., 1987; rep. 1989).

Strategies for Public Television in a Multichannel Environment – The Boston Consulting Group Study (Corporation for Public Broadcasting, Washington, D.C., March 1991).

Public Television and New Technologies

Monroe E. Price

Contents

1. The problem and aspiration 114
   1.1 Alternatives 115
   1.2 Leverage 116
2. Technology, vision, and structure 117
   2.1 Structural obstacles 119
   2.2 Technological possibilities 120
   2.3 Redefinition of functions 123
3. New technologies and their relationship to structure 124
   3.1 New technology as solution 125
   3.2 New technology and financing 126
   3.3 New technology and instruction 127
   3.4 New technology and national signal distribution 127
   3.5 New technology and the cultural function 128
   3.6 Technology and facilities 129
4. Federal policy 130
   4.1 New technology and funding 130
   4.2 New technology and flexibility of use 131
   4.3 Ancillary use 132
5. Structural obstacles to change 133
   5.1 Barriers to structural change 133
6. Changing structure and maximizing benefits
   from technology 137
7. A Carefully constructed auction 139
8. Conclusion 142

The argument of this chapter can be put simply: for *public broadcasting* to flourish, for new technologies to provide opportunities for substantial growth in impact, it may be necessary to transform *public broadcasters*. Institutions and entities of the industry have to change in ways that do not seem likely to occur. Indeed, the entire structure of public broadcasting, its history, its relationship to government, renders it relatively impervious to change. In antitrust policy, laws or decisions are often criticized because what they do is protect competitors not competition. Something similar is being argued here: the machinery and system in place, as we know it, is designed to protect the existing players rather than the function that is to be performed in American society. This chapter seeks to describe why this is the case and to recommend a dramatic way to alter the nature of the debate over public broadcasting's future.

1. The problem and aspiration

For much of the history of public television in the United States, the aspiration, indeed, the longing, for many has been for an entity that would look more like its European counterparts, especially the BBC. The dream (or envy) was for a public television that would become more of a force in society, that would have a larger audience, that would be capable of making a greater difference in terms of the specific goals that it has always articulated for itself. Instead, the reality of American public television has been turbulent and beset by structural problems, instability and insufficient funding. Its birthright, in fact, was a second-class technology. Now, however, technology has appeared as a possible lever for the accomplishment of submerged and all-but-forgotten goals.

For the reasons discussed in this chapter it is doubtful whether any of these opportunities for leverage will be used effectively to force those changes necessary to make public broadcasting more capable of using new technologies. Public broadcasters – like their commercial counterparts – want to preserve their present competitive position in the name of substantial change. They want to preserve most elements of the current structure but gain secure funding and more spectrum. It is like taking an old bungalow and pouring millions of dollars into it so that there is a more permanent, fixed and high-tech bungalow. The alternatives facing decisionmakers are to maintain the current mode of public broadcasting (with little or no change) or create or allow to be created greater conditions for internal readjustment. A third alternative, actively ending public broadcasting, has had some adherents, but is not considered an option here.

1.1 Alternatives

Maintaining the current mode is, with its modest changes, the most likely outcome even in the face of new technology. In this category belong the continuing debates over broadening or narrowing public broadcasting's ambit, activation of proposals to increase advertising, continued siphoning of major productions to new satellite-delivered channels, continued fights over federal funding, and the prospects for an endowment or guaranteed funding. Changes at the margin, by definition, mean preserving the existing institutions of public broadcasting but slowly diminishing its extended potential for contribution to the American public sphere.

The second alternative is creating or encouraging greater conditions for internal readjustment. Technology is already forcing this to some extent, but more is required for the rapid overhauling of institutional arrangements to assure that agreed-upon (if that is possible) goals of public broadcasting can be achieved. In large part, this means providing the legal and financial openness that would allow bidding and reward for further development of the assets of public broadcasting. These assets include the existing terrestrial distribution system including, in some markets, duplicative terrestrial distribution, existing contracts for satellite distribution, and potential spectrum rights. The premise of this alternative is that the kind of change necessary to maximize the value of new technologies cannot take place without major structural modification.

1.2 Leverage

There is a little leverage for change, namely, a desire of Congress to get out of the business of annual funding, and perhaps get out of the business of funding public broadcasting at all. Further, there is the leverage of the extraordinary need of public broadcasting for capital for transition to digital, almost $800 million in federal funds and $1.7 billion overall. There is the leverage at the FCC and at Congress finally to determine the rules that will govern access to and use of digitial spectrum. In addition, issues such as the way in which direct satellite broadcasters can satisfy their 4–7 percent requirement for informational and noncommercial programming can be used as leverage for change.

Without the careful marshalling of this leverage and more, technology will not lead to the kinds of changes necessary to substantially increase the role of public television in the United States. It would be a separate study to demonstrate that in broadcasting (and other industries) modes of adaptation to technology are a function, in large part, of industry structure. Aside from the initial flash of genius, the intuition of the founder, technological progress, so the hypothesis goes, is related to the risk-taking, decisionmaking capacity of a company. The capacity to take advantage of opportunities, to deploy capital, to innovate, all these are related to structure. A more modest hypothesis – and perhaps a sufficient one in the case of public broadcasting – is that certain forms of organization and internal decisionmaking are costly barriers to innovation. An organization that is conflicted between innovation and the protection of entities that are justifiable largely because of a particular status quo would be an example of a counter-technology environment. That does not mean that technology would not be implemented, but the pace and pattern of implementation would be unavoidably skewed.

The structure of U.S. public television – as described in the companion contributions to this volume of Mr. Somerset-Ward and Professor Rowland – retards substantially, the likelihood that it can take advantage of technological opportunities. As in the past with respect to other technologies, PBS and public broadcasting stations will take steps induced by technological opportunities, and that will lead to some systemic improvement, and perhaps that is all that can be anticipated. But the needs for change are so great and the opportunities presented so substantial, that more attention must be paid to bringing vision and possibilities into harmony.

2. Technology, vision, and structure

Technology, of course, is a key determinant of the moments and modes of transition. After all, public television, as it now exists in the United States, was, in its infancy, itself a social response to the availability of the new technology of television. Indeed, the history of public television could be written, in part, as the intersection of new media technology and government response. Upon the development of a Table of Allocations – the designation of spectrum for certain television users or licensees, the federal government reserved a portion (in some ways an orphan-like grab bag) of frequency opportunities for instructional and educational purposes. At that point, in the early 1950s, the essence of the reservation was the desire – at some point – to encourage entities that would adapt the then-new and potent technology of television to a specialized version of the public weal. The choice of colleges and universities, for the most part, as recipients of these licenses established and embedded a particular view of how public service television in the United States should proceed. From the very start, public policy involved a combination of engineering and organizational structure; and from the very beginning, this organizational structure had a substantial impact on the way in which the technology could be used. Public-service broadcasting would mirror, with a vengeance, the localism of its commercial counterpart.

Vision or purpose is inextricably tied to structure since all rational structures begin and end with the question of role and direction. For the emerging instructional sector, it would be another decade to fifteen years before the energy of major foundations, linked with high-level governmental concern, would lead to the Carnegie Commis-

117

sion report and a purposeful and comprehensive approach to the use of technology. The resulting system – the Corporation for Public Broadcasting, the Public Broadcasting Service and the ubiquitous local stations – have, since the mid-1960s adjusted or sought to adjust to additional new technologies. These have included the shift to color television, the mandate for improved reception of UHF signals, the use of the vertical blanking interval for closed captioning, the adjustment to cable television and the use of the satellite as a networking tool. Now, a complex, more comprehensive, more overwhelming set of technologies appear: the Internet, High-Definition Television, advanced television services, direct broadcasting services. Under federal legislation, all commercial and non stations will get a channel on which to broadcast DTV, consisting of either one HDTV program (and some datacasting) or multiple streams of standard definition programs and datacasting or other services. As was true in each earlier instance of engineering opportunity, the question is how the exisiting system adapts or alters as a result of a new technology and whether the system is organized so as best to use these new technologies.

Despite all the love and effort that went into its creation, from before the days of the first Carnegie Commission and up until the present day, the public broadcasting sector has been pressed into conflicting directions in terms of its mission and this is reflected in its structure. It is true that PBS and its member stations, and newer players like the American Programming Service, distribute a rich variety of educational programming to the public and to educational institutions using several means of distribution. It is true that PBS's National Program Service was gloriously a pioneer in distributing by satellite its programming for broadcast by PBS member stations and that it has been in the forefront in sending signals directly by direct broadcast satellite (DBS) services to areas unserved by local broadcast stations. The National Program Service is, as Somerset-Ward puts it, "the jewel in the crown" of PBS. Supplementing these are such offerings as PBS's Ready to Learn Service, an educational service offered in day care centers across the country that helps prepare preschoolers to enter kindergarten.

2.1 Structural obstacles

Yet, despite this overall positive face, there are deep problems, both horizontally and vertically, and these, too, are surveyed elsewhere in this volume. Horizontally, the confusion has been whether the system is driven by a social need for education and instruction – a need fired by the great demands of a huge, overburdened collection of elementary and high schools throughout the country – or whether it is an instrument for cultural programming, to bring the riches of the metropolis to the entire nation and to bring the diverse cultures of the American people to each other. There has been, at times, a division over whether public-service broadcasting is an instrument primarily for the broad center and the major cultural institutions that serve it or, in addition, one specifically designed to redress lacunae by programming for the cultural needs of underserved groups in society. Finally, in recent years (and reflecting a debate in public-service broadcasting systems globally) an additional question has arisen if competitive entertainment programming ought to be part of a diet that makes cultural offerings more palatable, improving overall ratings. Of course, it can be all of these: opera and symphonies, foreign language programming, programming that helps the diverse groups in society understand their own needs better and programming that informs and enriches all by increasing knowledge generally. But all – doing everything – is costly, in terms of resources, and in terms of fashioning strategy.

This horizontal problem is compounded by the competitive environment in which public broadcasting finds itself. What was formerly a niche which PBS held exclusively is now chipped away by competing cable programming services and this may be far more the case in a digital future. Cultural channels, however imperfect at the moment, dilute an audience for classical music and adventurous films. Internet providers and competing cable educational services challenge PBS' dominance in classroom instruction. And, as PBS changes programming to capture and retain an audience, it becomes slightly more like the commercial channels from which it seeks to differentiate itself. Finally new technologies, multicast channels resulting from expanded spectrum availability and digital compression, abundant channels promised by cable and telephone competitors, and even the Internet, present competition for that most valuable of commodities, viewer time.

Vertically, the American system is also structurally riven. There is, most famously, the ancient division over whether the system is national, with local nodes, or local with national coordination. Here the structural flaws have the greatest consequences. Nationally, there is the complexity created by the existence of both the Corporation and Public Broadcasting Service. Within PBS, there are conflicts between the large and powerful stations and others over who should control decisions and how to use new technologies. *Quality Time* argued that structural flaws meant that scarce funds that are expended on maintaining a complex system of local stations and station managements could better be spent on a national programming service with greater production and more elaborate marketing. Intersector competition intensifies the problems inherent in structure. A divided PBS, with conflicts between center and stations, must compete with cable programming services, commercial networks and international providers (like the BBC) that are highly integrated. These fault lines have been widening, and with debilitating consequences, for three decades.

2.2 Technological possibilities

New technology becomes an occasion, in most healthy organizations, to rethink opportunities, and the same has been the case for public broadcasting. Take, for example, the expansion of spectrum made available in the 1996 Telecommunications Act to commercial broadcasters. Vice-President Gore, in an October, 1997 ceremony announcing an Advisory Committee on Public-Interest Obligations for Digital TV renewed a possibility for using technology to benefit the public broadcasters. Speaking of the commercial television system that controls the bulk of the audience, he said that "[The] tradition of trusteeship must continue, even as television goes through the greatest transformation in its history, one that is truly bigger than the shift from black and white to color – the move from analogue to

120

digital broadcasting." But a subtext was that "public-interest" obligations could be satisfied in part by payment to public broadcasters from their commercial counterparts.

"We also know," Vice-President Gore continued, "that digital broadcasting will be more dynamic and more flexible; more competitive and more interactive – and potentially much more responsive to the needs and interests of the American people, if we prepare for it in the right way ... [T]he fact that [the new technology] is so limitless – the fact that so many of our present rules and expectations will not apply – makes digital broadcasting the wild west of the television age. If we don't map out some of that terrain for public purposes – if we don't carve out meaningful public space on our newest public airwaves – we could lose the opportunity for good."

Here the tones of the past are reiterated: the notion of reservations, the idea that a portion of spectrum should be set aside and provided to those who have been the guardians of public broadcasting in the past. This, too, seems to be a hallmark of the existing U.S. approach. Advanced television service should be and will be brought to us by those who brought its analogue predecessors. Vice-President Gore employed a theme which suggests the relationship between technology, structure and opportunity: "At the same time, the digital spectrum is a valuable asset, one that will bring an explosion of opportunities for broadcasters. What we have asked for in return – what we must get in return – is a significant commitment to the public-interest. We all know what the critical needs are: the need to educate and inform our children; the need to give parents the tools to protect their children from what they consider to be harmful influences; the need for free and open political debate, driven not by dollars and soundbites, but by issues and ideas. The challenge we now face is meeting those needs, protecting our oldest values, in the face of new and changing technology ..."

This statement involves a special opportunity – related to structure – in American broadcasting. The question, embedded in Gore's political rhetoric, is whether commercial broadcasters, provided with extremely valuable spectrum, can be required to disgorge some of the benefits which they will gain and (this being the part relating to the structure of public broadcasting) whether this dividend – if it comes to pass – will be assigned to or seized by the public television system. The issue is not only the internal capacity of public television to develop a strategy, but also the relationship of structure to politics, and the capacity of PBS and the lobbying arm of the local stations to make their power felt.

In terms of vision, or official understanding of purpose, the Federal Communications Commission, in its Fourth Report on advanced television services and digital spectrum, put it the following way in terms of the role that public broadcasting plays and the regulatory steps that are necessary in a time of new technology to allow it to expand its role:

> We note our commitment to noncommercial educational television service and our recognition of the high-quality programming service noncommercial stations have provided to American viewers over the years. We also acknowledge the financial difficulties faced by noncommercial stations and reiterate our view that noncommercial stations will need and warrant special relief measures to assist them in the transition to DTV [ditigal television]. Accordingly, we intend to grant such special treatment to noncommercial broadcasters to afford them every opportunity to participate in the transition to digital television, and we will deal with them in a lenient manner ... [W]e wish to note that public broadcasting service was the first to establish a digital satellite transmission system and that public broadcasting licensees are in the forefront of experimenting with digital television.

The indications are that public television will be in the forefront in terms of using additional capacity to experiment with High-Definition Television, perhaps being more experimental and more in advance than the commercial stations. But this could mean that public broadcasting will be the undercompensated stalking horse for commercial television. Public television could provide, through HDTV, an inducement for the purchase of advanced sets at a time when it is not economic to do so for the commercial stations, but not receive any substantial benefit for its pioneering role.

2.3 Redefinition of functions

One anticipation is that technology will aid in resolving the problem of what PBS is, what functions it best serves. To be sure, some re-definition will occur: technology requires it because of the way adaptation to technology means taking structures apart and putting them back again. But technology does not obviate choice: the new technology has the appearance of abundance but it will certainly be the case that public television cannot do all things or perform best by trying to continue and intensify all of its prior goals.

Because, notwithstanding dreams, not everything can be done, it is necessary to look at the variety of possible definitions for public television. Among these are the following:

Lifeline
Under this definition, public service television takes on the residue of public-interest obligations from commercial broadcasting, whatever they are. Under some proposals, and the Children's Television Act of 1990 can serve as a model, commercial broadcasters, in the new technology future, could shed public-interest responsibilities if they were willing to pay noncommercial broadcasters to assume them in their stead. The President has established a National Advisory Committee for Public-Interest and the Digital Spectrum that has fifteen members – taken from industry, the public and politics – that will report by June, 1998 what standards ought to be imposed or transferred.

National treasure, national identity
This definition is a reminder of the BBC and European public television in its orgins, in which the institution is, in terms of a cultural role, overarching, like the monarchy, a secular version of the Church of England, bearer and reflector of identity and charged with a conscious strategic role in changing culture. This social role is, more than the merely attaining viewers, enough to justify a license fee. This model is rarely the one that is used to express public television in the United States, and public broadcasting has not evolved a sufficient audience share to perform this role.

Minority satisfaction or empowerment model
The best example of this, outside Channel 4 in the United Kingdom, is SBS in Australia. In Australia, the network is dedicated to Vietnamese, Indian, and other minority culture films and similar, conscious counter-programming with the intent that diverse groups deem themselves more meaningfully included in the Australian whole. The U.S. public broadcasting service performs this function to some extent, but when it does it in too notorious a way, it becomes charged with ignoring its mainstream acculturating or reinforcing responsibility.

Public sphere
Another way of looking at purpose is to say the public service broadcasting is an instrument of civil society, part of the creation of a public sphere. It increasingly takes on this function as the commercial entities in American television abandon that role more and more. Perhaps it will have a ceded monopoly on certain public events – like political conventions and presidential and regional and local television debates.

The collection of activities called public broadcasting
A reasonable alternative is not to wax philosophical, but to recognize that there is an existing structure with existing practices and existing institutional neuroses and goals. What that existing structure is, and how it marginally extends itself is what constitutes public broadcasting in the United States.

3. New technologies and their relationship to structure

The principal new technology, the technology that is forcing decisions, involves providing additional spectrum for advanced television services. This technology alone is causing important planning shifts within PBS. But other new technologies and PBS' attitude towards them include the Internet and the new patterns in global distribution of television signals. In this section, the attitude toward new technologies and the steps being taken or under consideration are evaluated in terms of the existing problems of structure. PBS and local stations are doing much to adjust to new technologies, in terms of using on-line services, developing revenue streams from the sale of video-casettes, aggressively entering the world of High-Definition Television and planning multiple channels made possible through digitalization and compression of signals. These wholly laudable emblems of an emboldened PBS must be put in context.

3.1 New technology as solution

New technology can be perceived – and this is sometimes a great danger – as a providential way out of an entity's historic conceptual difficulties. This is a particular danger for PBS. New technologies are thought to be a way of solving old horizontal and vertical problems. Take the horizontal problems discussed above. Digitalization and compression mean that newly available spectrum can be used for multicasting. Because of newly abundant capacity, it is thought, the system can transcend its functional ambivalences by encompassing everything. It can be both a great cultural broadcaster and a targeted provider of educational and instructional programming. It can be a channel for the mainstream and for the edges. It can be politically centrist and politically daring. That is the dream. Technology relieves scarcity; and scarcity, not the complexity of defining purpose, can be deemed the source for prior dilemmas.

A similar approach is possible to the "vertical" problems. Because of the technology of national direct broadcasting, the tortured structural past can have a happy "both/and" solution as well. Technology, here forces, or is thought to force a solution, though here it is technology linked, as always, with legislation or regulation. The 1992 Cable Act requires direct broadcast services to set aside 4–7 percent of their capacity for programming akin to that of public television. If PBS and the local stations want to gain this opportunity, they have to fashion a national feed that is unmediated by local and regional outlets and it appears that this will occur.

Both of these hopes – solutions to the vertical and horizontal problems, the problems of vision and purpose and the internal crippling issues of structure – are not, however, automatically resolved by the existence of technology. Both solutions, and this is their weakness, are linked to funding. This is true especially of the horizontal questions of niche programming versus comprehensive appeal. But it is true of the second, as well, since legislative provisions that have structural implications come bound in budget packages. How funds are obtained, both in amount or in process, will determine what impact technology has on public television.

3.2 New technology and financing

This is, of course, the well-rehearsed problem of scope of funding and reliability of funding. Multicasting means a great call on production. Transition to advanced television services, including HDTV, requires new equipment. PBS has just emerged, as the Rowland chapter painstakingly describes, from conflict in federal funding and problems in subscriber and underwriter support. The result is that new technology is being invoked to resolve this third and encompassing problem of the system: the political pull of annual funding as opposed to the relative comfort of a sustained source of revenue, either through a license fee or endowment or predetermined annual payment.

Increasingly, new technology is positioned as a lever to solve this problem. Income streams rising from digital spectrum might be tapped for public broadcasting or assets sold to create an endowment. The important thing is that, here too, unresolved issues, deeply and historically divisive, can be overcome by the arrival of expanded technical capabilities. Thus, the most important part of a tentative, sketchy but powerful suggestion of Vice-President Gore is that funds from commercial broadcasters, possibly relieved of other public-interest obligations, might be made available for public service broadcasters. This is also, as will be seen below, the direction urged by Congressman Billy Tauzin, chair of the Congressional committee most concerned with these issues.

3.3 New technology and instruction

Before these structural issues are discussed further, it is useful to indicate how new technologies could be used conventionally to assist in the performance of the system's function. Public broadcasting is, of course, the nation's primary source of classroom programming, reaching 30 million students in kindergarten through 12th grade and 2 million teachers in 70,000 schools. It claims to be the world's leader in college telecourses because over 2.6 million adults have earned college credit through the PBS Adult Learning Service. PBS claims a distance learning program in which several technologies are used: broadcast, cable, satellite and video-cassette and disc, and through the PBS ONLINE Website. PBS is proud of its history of being the first, in the United States, to use technology to develop closed captioning for the hearing impaired, descriptive video services for the visually impaired, and stereo television services; and to transmit television programming by satellite. As indicated above, technology, particularly the technology of multicasting, is to be used to increase greatly the service's commitment to instruction and education. The president of PBS, Ervin Duggan, has promised that a return to education and instruction seems a clearly important part of a multicasting future as well as a politically acceptable use of some significant aspect of the abundance made possible through new technology.

3.4 New technology and national signal distribution

A key element of the "both/and" solution is the enhancement of a PBS-controlled national broadcasting service. A direct to home service that would bypass intermediate stations seems to be a significant symbolic part of such a solution. After its fall 1997 annual meeting, PBS announced it would provide a direct feed to DBS operators for transmission to all DBS subscribers, not only those unserved by a local PBS signal. This was a major step by PBS since the signal would be national in origin and distribution. Furthermore, the announcement was significant in indicating some progress in terms of internal structure. The membership, composed of local stations, voted to proceed with this approach despite reluctance and in contrast to blocking efforts by stations in previous years. The possibility of such a national signal meant that PBS simultaneously sought a Congressional amendment to the Satellite Home Viewer Act to facilitate the automatic clearance of copyright restrictions to be delivered through a national signal.

3.5 New technology and the cultural function

One of the most significant challenges to PBS is how to maintain its franchise as cultural consciousness, or at least the television custodian of that consciousness. Ever since CBS sought – unsuccessfully and too early – to develop a high cultural alternative to PBS, this aspect of the programming strategy has been at risk. Now with planned pay channels like Horizon, with the History Channel and Arts & Entertainment, with Bravo on the arts cinema front, the unrealized threat of CBS may be partly accomplished. It is possible that competition has increased the viewership of such programming, but not significantly, especially given data that viewership in general has remained static despite the jump in the number of choices.

PBS is trying to address this in part through multicasting and the new technology. It would repackage its cultural programming, possibly seeking to do more to differentiate itself from the competition. Under its announced plan for a digital future PBS would show many of the network's prime-time shows, such as "Nova," and "Great Performances," or "Masterpiece Theater," in wide screen and high definition with accompanying six-channel enhanced digital sound. During other day-parts, PBS stations would divide their digital channel, splitting it into four channels, offering, as an example, children's programming on one channel, an adult-education show on another, a nature show on a third and elementary-school course work on the fourth. Using the multichannel option, PBS stations would have the ability to offer children's programming and adult cultural programming simultaneously.

In a digital multichannel future, PBS is considering that viewers might first negotiate a menu screen with small windows – one for each available channel, so they could then select which to watch. In addition, the expanded technology would mean that a portion of the spectrum would be used to send data to viewers, such as teacher guides for teachers.

3.6 Technology and facilities

Already, small steps are being taken toward the digital and multi-casting future. In October 1997, the Public Broadcasting Service dedicated its new all-digital technical operations center (TOC). It had been the decision of Ervin Duggan, president of PBS, to demonstrate the Service's dedication to technology by being on the "bleeding edge" of transition to digital broadcasting. PBS had begun digital transmissions on a limited basis in 1994, providing dual analogue and digital feed for months, and switched to all-digital path to air in the fall of 1996. At the ceremony establishing the center, Duggan and other PBS officials said that the switch to digital "positions PBS for the next step" to High-Definition Television and that it helped PBS "double or triple the number of our feeds, [the signals provided to local stations] probably at lower cost than 5 years ago." The early switch was consistent with PBS' history "of getting there first" and "our desire to be on the cutting edge." He said PBS was able to add new technology quicker than commercial broadcasters because "we are not so driven by commercial imperatives" and because manufacturers were willing to provide discounts to get their equipment placed in a high-profile public-service operation.

4. Federal policy

4.1 New technology and funding

As mentioned, given the existing structure (and even without it), a vital element of any solution is more reliable, less politicized federal funding. Without such funding, technology alternatives do not provide the possibility of break through solutions. The technology of abundance without a strategy to program for it and without annual, politically-sensitive funding efforts is but a chimera. Representative W. J. "Billy" Tauzin, chairman of the House Commerce telecommunications subcommittee, has been advancing a plan, announced in September 1997, in which commercial broadcasters might establish a fund or provide annual payments for public television uses in exchange for burden-free licenses to develop High-Definition Television (HDTV). This solution, often bruited about in the past, would provide a benefit even over license fee models. The plan has many advocates, but it is so ambitious, it so removes from Congress the blood sport of punching at PBS annually, that its chances for success are only fair.

Under the plan, the argument could be made – and has been by Congressman Tauzin – that "taxpayers would no longer have to help pay their [public television's] bills." The Congressman has also stated plans to form a commission – parallelling one established by the White House – that would study other new ways to fund public broadcasting. Under the plan, commercial broadcasters would have the option to subsidize public television further rather than air required children's programming or offer free political air time, mirroring options included in the 1990 children's television legislation. A forerunner of the Tauzin proposal[1], sponsored by former Senator

---

1 In early October, 1997, CPB forwarded to the White House an implementation proposal which underscored the importance of a financing plan. At issue was the question of how much it would cost public television stations to make the transition to advance services, digitalization and HDTV. CPB requested $771 million in federal funds – over and above the usual operating budget – to help pay for the change. This $771, and $1 billion more that would be raised by local stations, would be in addition to the endowment for operations that would be the subject of the Tauzin fund.

Larry Pressler, sought to establish a trust endowment for public broadcasting in 1995 that would have been funded in part by auctioning off HDTV airwaves. The bill died after Congress decided to give broadcasters the HDTV spectrum for free.

4.2 New technology and flexibility of use

For public broadcasting – as for its commercial counterpart – one of the most pressing immediate strategic questions is how the new spectrum resource will be used. While High-Definition Television was the promise that induced much Congressional interest in providing spectrum to existing broadcasters, incumbents, both public and private, want flexibility so that they can maximize the benefit of what is obtained. The FCC has, however, begun to constrain, slightly, those available alternatives. In the Fourth Further Notice/Third Inquiry on Advanced Television Services, the FCC outlined its policy goals both for noncommercial and commercial television: they included "1) preserving a free, universal broadcasting service; 2) fostering an expeditious and orderly transition to digital technology that will allow the public to receive the benefits of digital television while taking account of consumer investment in NTSC television sets; 3) managing the spectrum to permit the recovery of contiguous blocks of spectrum, so as to promote spectrum efficiency and to allow the public the full benefit of its spectrum; and 4) ensuring that the spectrum – both ATV channels and recovered channels – will be used in a manner that best serves the public-interest." Put more simply, the FCC has as a primary goal the promotion and preservation of a free, universally available, local broadcast television in a digital world.

Just as it used the "must-carry" rule to strengthen broadcasting at a time of severe competition from cable, it now seeks to ensure a smooth transition by providing existing licensees with additional spectrum and imposing certain simulcasting requirements. Simultaneously, by setting limits for the transition, or providing, in other ways, some idea of transition, the Commission was seeking "to promote spectrum efficiency and rapid recovery of spectrum."

4.3 Ancillary use

Public broadcasters might have taken the position – consistent with FCC goals – that all new spectrum they obtained would be used for educational, cultural and informational uses and that such uses would be free to viewers. Instead, the primary associations of public broadcasters told the FCC that they favor something that gives them the opportunity to raise funds from this new spectrum. They would be free to provide ancillary broadcast and nonbroadcast use of the DTV channel, supporting the Commission's position that "flexible use will serve the public-interest by helping to spur development of new technologies and to provide greater opportunities for noncommercial stations to enhance their public service to their respective communities."

Under the public television position, these services could serve noncommercial and revenue producing purposes. Obviously, "a noncommercial station could ... utilize digital transmission to distribute program-related course materials, textbooks, student and teacher guides, computer software and content areas of the World Wide Web as part of the station's instructional programming." But it would also be true that "noncommercial stations could use ancillary and supplementary services, without regard to the educational content, as a revenue source to support nonprofit services and operations and the transition to DTV."[2] Public stations could launch a pay service or otherwise use some portion of their new capacity to raise revenues for the remainder of their efforts. PBS and the Association of America's Public Television Stations (AAPTS), the licencees lobbying group, also opposed a requirement of a minimum time or capacity commitment to High-Definition Television, rather leaving that determination to the marketplace. AAPTS and PBS, in joint comments, opposed a minimum HDTV requirement, noting that the Commission "can rely on broadcasters and public television's commitment to HDTV." They argued that if the Commission adopts an

---

2 In the Matter of Advanced Television Systems and their Impact Upon the Existing Television Broadcast Service; MM Docket No. 87-268; 62 FR 26966; Federal Communications Commission; 1997 FCC Lexis 4007; 7 Comm. Reg. (P & F) 863; Release-Number: FCC 97-116; April 21, 1997 Released; Adopted April 3, 1997.

HDTV requirement, it should be "liberally waived" for noncommercial stations (particularly those analogue stations that may share a DTV channel in the transition).

5. Structural obstacles to change

These responses and adaptations to the availability of spectrum for advanced television services are examples of how public television, like every other institution in American society, is affected profoundly by the existence of new technologies. The central idea here, however, is that new technologies are a relatively small variable in terms of the future of public television in the United States. Of course, public television will change – and will have to change. But technological change will not, and certainly not alone, materially alter the market share or impact or global status of the American service. It will alter public television – no doubt – but it cannot provide the miraculous cure that seems to be anticipated as the PBS system looks to new technology to help resolve the problem of definition of function, to resolve long-standing disputes about the national versus local nature of the system and, as well, to open the door to more secure funding. Let me examine each of these in turn:

5.1 Barriers to structural change

The remainder of this chapter will focus on what was called the second alternative at the beginning of this chapter: creating the conditions for change, adaptation and major shifts in institutional structures to permit better use of new technologies. In the absence of such change, there is slow decay and death as PBS program niches get picked away, or marketplace adaptation by which PBS becomes more like another cable programming service with a respectable narrowcasting share.

To look at structural obstacles to change, we must look at elements of the status quo and their effect on innovation. For example, PBS has obtained, through the must-carry rule, a Congressional guarantee of shelf space on cable (and, to a much shakier extent, on DBS), shielding it from certain of the competitive pressures of that new technology. While other services, like Discovery and Bravo, were pressured to determine their role in a multichannel environment, public broadcasting could maintain the status quo. Thus cable guaranteed it an expanded market, for a time, rather than merely creating a multichannel environment in which it would do worse. Even the initiation of C-Span by the cable industry had its soporific effect on public broadcasting: while this entity can be viewed as a competitor to public broadcasting, it can also be perceived as an entity that relieved PBS of some public sphere obligations.

In short, public broadcasting has been protected from market pressures felt elsewhere that might have forced greater internal structural changes and led to greater transformation of its programming strategy. It has not had to change to keep cable channel position and to convince cable operators to carry the signal. By the same token, the protection of existing broadcast stations meant that the system did not, at an early stage, build a cable programming channel, as ABC and NBC did.

Similarly, in a period of intense jockeying for position in a global market, the existing clumsy internal organizational structure, coupled with the history of public broadcasting, has meant that U.S. public broadcasting will not be a major player, as a national entity, in transnational services. This does not mean that WNET or WGBH will not make deals and money. Here the focus is whether there is a market for an internationalized American public television as an entity. Technology makes such a market possible, but not for the U.S. system. The major commercial competitors in the global marketplace are American, but U.S. public broadcasting has no significant role. It is the BBC that is trying to stake out a global identity or increase its global trademark for the Anglophone market.

There are several reasons for this: public broadcasting in the U.S. was never strong in news, and competition in news seems to be one of the most important areas for global competition. The BBC effort which at first was a mixture of news and entertainment, seems now to be wholly news and information. One can ask, as well, whether the internal and public pressure on PBS, particularly in news and public affairs, has been toward the local and, therefore, the parochially domestic, while the BBC has always had a product which was more transnational and regional or global. Second, PBS never really developed an international consumer brand name recognition that could compete with the BBC. The internal organization of PBS means that it is not nearly so equipped to have an external strategy as is the BBC. Besides, within the great tent of the BBC, an external voice was always a vital and distinguished part. In the U.S., the Voice of America was always kept away from public broadcasting. The British way was not necessarily preferable, only that it was far more natural for the BBC to have an international agenda – and to know the territory – than for PBS, despite its international marketing and co-production deals.

It is possible, as one model for the future, that there will be a global public service (or one Anglophone, one Francophone) with national affiliates. The question is whether there is a global alliance to make this happen and whether the national or local entities are so public-sphere driven that such a model would be hard to create. Related is the idea that there could be a kind of global arts and cultural television production alliance, with a national focus on public sphere activities. One interesting aspect has been the development of a strategic arrangement between the BBC and Discovery Channel for certain global programming (and domestic production) rather than extending a more exclusive relationship with the U.S. public broadcasting system.

These are then two big areas where technology affects public broadcasting: the impact of cable television and the direct broadcast satellite (DBS) in terms of fashioning the domestic market, and the role of satellites in developing a global market.

PBS' own history provides impediments to vital change. There is no library to speak of since the independent producers retain library rights, no effective international alliance, no dominating history that public broadcasting has a central role in national identity building, no tradition of a license, and a creaky structure which protects itself from innovation by buffering itself against job loss and extinction.

Some of the changes necessary to alter the capacity of the public system to take advantage of new technologies have been implemented, and new technologies have been used to produce these changes. A New Technologies Working Group (NTWG) has been established and converted to a PBS board committee. President Duggan told his board that the effort was to ensure that the NTWG formed under his direction in 1994 would be "more secure" as it pursued its mission on DBS and other issues, such as digital TV. It was precisely such governance reforms which seemed to make technology-positive decisions easier to adopt. For example, the vote on direct feeds occurred after PBS's first-ever membership meeting, a result of February 1997 reforms. The vote arose on the resolution of a coalition of stations urging that PBS be "position[ed] to take advantage of DBS channels set aside," referring to the proposed 4–7 percent set aside for noncommercial educational programming on DBS services in the 1992 Cable Act.

Prior to this vote, and the governance reforms, PBS stations consistently voiced concern that a national feed would in fact compete against them. They argued that a national-feed DBS channel would have unfair advantages over local stations. The national feed might have a superior picture to that of the local station. By making DBS more acceptable, by contributing to its appeal to subscribers, PBS would be enhancing a system where switch-back to terrestrial uses might be hindered and local stations impaired. As an example of this station-based reluctance, one member station sought to have the future DBS feed be "distinct" from National Program Service (NPS) programming. Assurances had to be given that the feed be differentiated and, as a consequence, harm to local stations would be minimized. Furthermore, if there were fundraising on the national feed, the proceeds would be returned to stations in the donor's zip code.

At the same time, in a development perhaps linked to issues of technology, the chair of PBS, Gerald Baliles, publicly stated that PBS's governance structure needed to be changed "to outfit ourselves for that new future." He said "we don't have time to waste," and since the launch of the governance review process last fall, PBS has heard from "many" within the system who are pro-change. He recognized that those favoring a stronger, more efficient PBS consistently complained that the existing board structure and complicated decisionmaking process made it impossible. Even those who favored a tighter arrangement had expressed doubt about whether PBS was the entity that ought to be the carrier of renewed leadership. Reflecting the ambivalence toward the issue, Baliles was later quoted as saying to a closed governance panel that structural change might not be necessary, and suggesting a go-slow approach.

6. Changing structure and maximizing benefits from technology

Looking at all this from another angle, one can ask what impact the new technologies have had on existing broadcasting entitities and how they have positioned themselves to exploit these opportunities. That would provide some suggestion of whether public television is properly organized (on the assumption that other, more commercial entities have behaved in a rational manner). New technologies have, of course, facilitated the creation of a completely different environment worldwide. Quite obviously, and this became true with cable and satellite and now with digital spectrum, the transformation has been from few channels to an abundance of them. It has moreover meant a substantial shift from a television system that was all free (advertising supported or public) to one in which payments by the viewer to a distributor (or direct to a programmer) has become prevalent. From this, a new industry organization of gatekeepers and distribution patterns has emerged. New technologies have meant the possibility, and then the inevitability, of cheaper cross-border distribution and therefore the possibility of global markets. This, too, has meant redefinitions of strategies by programmers and by distributors of programming. And the final new technology, the Internet and World Wide Web, has altered – and continues to alter – the amount, method and form of information coming from broadcaster to consumer.

The creation of a greater number of channels and the fundamental change in the distribution systems in the United States has had a sharply differentiated impact on commercial and noncommercial television in the United States. For much of commercial broadcasting, this technology-driven fact has led to strategies of consolidation and vertical integration, neither of which has characterized the public television sector. There is no PBS equivalent of the Disney acquisition of ABC or of the Time Warner merger with Turner. The multichannel opportunities of cable have meant that existing commercial players have developed new products, like CNBC, MSNBC, ESPN, and A & E. Public television has not developed similar products during the last twenty years. It has mainly maintained its niche in a time of economic, political and cultural assault. This is not a point of chastisement, just description. Given all the political turmoil that public television has faced, maintaining and slightly improving the status quo is more than could have been expected.

As to the altered global landscape, because of the never-ending need of the commercial networks to extend and expand markets, coupled with a library of programs to which they own rights and the desire to develop brand name recognition, large, relatively untapped, potentially consumer-oriented markets have been increasingly attractive. Not only NBC, Murdoch, Sony and others have been willing to take large risks to establish audiences using new satellite technology coupled with new multichannel terrestrial distribution systems (or DTH). The BBC has been aggressive as well. Its strategy explicitly has been to become more secure at home and more competitive worldwide. Public television has not had the leisure or the resources or the organization to engage such a dual strategy. In the current political environment, it had to focus on domestic issues and there was not the Congressional support for investment in PBS to take great overseas risks. For the BBC (and a few other state-supported public broadcasting services), the government has seen it as in its interest to make investments that will either help the national policy cause abroad or pay off and mean less reliance on the domestic license fee.

7. A carefully constructed auction

In this environment of great technological opportunity and dogged structural and political impediments, a number of more radical approaches have been suggested. Lawrence Grossman's proposal for a high-powered second public network, utilizing prime time in a portion of the week, with advertising support, is discussed in Dean Rowland's chapter. Somerset-Ward, in his chapter, suggests a variety of steps that would lead to more consolidation, greater investment in programming production, and more rational use of existing assets. The enterprising PBS president, Ervin Duggan, has his own publicly stated agenda for progress in streamlining within the existing framework of public television.

One more aggressive approach is for there to be an auction of the national service, along the lines of the British ITV auctions, where there is a described set of functions to be performed. Bidders offer to perform the required functions or bid up the functions to be performed. Bids would contain – depending on the nature of the functions described or the proposal of the contenders – either a payment to the government or the guarantee of the services promised for a contracted government contribution. The full design of such an auction – too ambitious for this chapter – can serve as a mental exercise in subjecting public television to carefully selected market pressures, not the accidental ones that now affect program policies adversely.

Public service television – or more likely some part of it – would be spun off into a private or semi-private corporation, much like the privatization of airports or highways or the operation of prisons or schools. This technique is used as a means of forcing a definition of purpose and trying to obtain a more efficient way of accomplishing national goals. The technique is also used as a way of limiting or defining the government contribution to a public enterprise. Looking at the evolution of public television globally, no system has used exactly this approach. On the other hand, public television globally seems to be moving from state control to a more public-private partnership or towards entities more capable of competing in a multichannel and globally defined environment. In surprising ways, the former evolution of the state broadcasters in Central and Eastern Europe and in Russia have hallmarks of such a redefinition.

To help understand this auction approach, one could ask who the bidders might be. Looking at counterpart commercial restructurings, candidates might include those who are central to the existing system or an entity with a library and production capability that could use a public distribution system. An auction would increase the likelihood of vertical or horizontal integration in the various markets of which public television is a part. It is unclear who all the bidders might be, but some possibilities include the Children's Television Workshop or PBS itself or a BBC-Discovery consortium or an alliance of major PBS local stations, alone or with the BBC. A commercial network like CBS seeking to redefine itself, might participate in such an auction, or Disney-ABC.

It is impossible, in this chapter, to indicate exactly how such an auction would be structured to render technological opportunities more productive, in terms of the goals of a public service, but some indication is possible. One idea would be to establish a bidding process for prime-time public broadcasting – the National Programming Service – but leave the remainder to local affiliates. Extremely important would be whether the bidder would have some portion of the multicasting opportunities available as a result of spectrum expansion and digital compression and under what conditions. As an example, the bidder would be committed to providing an "as is or better" public broadcast system to close to 100 percent of U.S. households with some right to do limited advertising on PBS stations and some obligation to provide a new public broadcasting channel on cable to something like the SBS or Channel 4 model. The bidder could also bid by providing funds for the use by affiliates during day programs. The bidder would provide a plan for the use of digital spectrum and local broadcasting stations would be required to clear prime time. The bid would be similar to the British system for the award of Channel 5 licenses and the award being for a period of years with a new bid at the end (as opposed to a license renewal process). Congress could still participate by creating additional program development funds, or by funding major cultural institutions to produce programming with the successor organization.

While a great temptation and likelihood would arise, it would be highly pragmatic for entities that might seek to enter into such an auction to help define its terms. This determination should be done through hearings before the Federal Communications Commission or before a Congressional subcommittee. An auction or similar transaction might, for example, mean that proceeds from a privatized national service, including use of digital spectrum during prime time, would finance local entities with a redefined function as well as production. Federal budgetary contributions might, in the future, be limited to support for educational or instructional offerings. One bidder might offer to provide a service like SBS in Australia which spoke specifically to under-served language minorities in the United States. Funds from an auction could be used to support local production by local public broadcasting entities during those periods not reserved for those who prevail at auction. There could be an auction for a nationally-based but decentralized distance learning Program (like Ready to Learn), in which the bidder proposed a model for utilizing available digital spectrum, reservations on direct broadcast satellites, and over terrestrial facilities. Such a bid might be contingent on funding, or promise some version of partial self-funding through tuition and other revenue-producing methods. The function of opening up possibilities – of allowing Microsoft or Disney or the BBC or Children's Television Workshop (or a combination of the major PBS stations) to make a bid would be to allow a reconceptualization to occur which did not depend, for its initial validity, on the protection of existing entities. The British Open University might participate in a bid for post-secondary instructional broadcasting, in conjunction with a consortium of American universities or with the Learning Channel.

The idea, here, is only to sketch the possibilities. It is an understatement to say that there are enormous, probably insurmountable, hurdles. These would include coordinating a carved out role with the continuing existence of local station licensees, the constitutional questions involved in actually determining what a public broadcasting entity should do, the difficult question of who would judge among bidders and by what criteria. It is only because of some structural approach that might substantially reenergize – even more than is now occurring – and strengthen public broadcasting that such a complex suggestion is put forward.

8. Conclusion

Ervin Duggan is a leader who uses formal opportunities to try to build consensus or the appearance of consensus. In a June 1996 speech, Duggan gave an important view of the relationship between structure and technological development. Instead of reflecting on fracture and dissent, an earlier theme, Duggan announced a "year of victory," of "solidarity, unity and cohesion." He wished to dispel concerns of local stations that PBS wished to become independent of them, rather than tied to their continued maintenance. "Let there be no ambiguity," Duggan exhorted. "We know why we are here. PBS is here to serve you. We cannot reach our audience except through you." In the speech, Duggan specifically addressed PBS efforts in the area of new technologies. Duggan pointed to the PBS World Wide Web site and the formation of the New Technologies Working Group originally charged with examining the prospects of HDTV, Advanced TV and DBS for programmers and stations.

Many of these are important steps. They will yield improvements in the workings of the public broadcasting services. They do so, however, within a structure that remains hobbled. The emphasis on structure in this chapter is based on the assumption that exploitation of technology in the public-interest depends on a complex of political and structural forces. In a world in which there is intense reorganization so as to maximize the potential gains from technology shifts, the greatest danger to public television could be an inability to react adequately to opportunities provided. It is in this context that a number of suggestions have been made for moderate and radical change as precursors for the benefits of engineering advancement. Of course, *ex ante*, it is difficult to know what changes in structure will lead to particular social benefits. It may well be that a highly decentralized and almost atomized system can be a greater goad for change than one that is more structured and controlled from above. The early results from the commercial sector are mixed. But it is clear that the investments, the flexibility and the speed necessary for change to take advantage of new technologies require structural change in public television. New technologies are, in a sense, like new playing cards dealt in a high-stakes game. They are opportunities to be sure; but they are deeply embedded in a pre-existing context and a complex competitive environment. Technologies create opportunities, but policymakers, legislators, managers and citizens provide the environment and structures in which those technologies manifest themselves. Technological determinism has its place in the discourse of history; but in the corner of public broadcasting, at this moment in time, it is implementation, not the technology itself, which is most fateful.

At a time when huge commercial networks have been gobbled up, have transformed or virtually disintegrated, where relations between networks and affiliates have been in a state of constant flux, where the relationships among industry components – broadcasters and cable, for example – have gone from prohibited to intimate, public broadcasting should be subject to radical reexamination as well. Yet, public broadcasting – the entities of public broadcasting – are holier cows than their British counterpart. The pressure on the BBC to transform, to act competitively and to alter, substantially, its structure so as to function in the next several decades, has been dramatic and effective. For all the clumsy and culture-laden debate about public-broadcasting in the United States, for all the oaths and cataclysmic predictions from the public broadcasting community or harsh pledges of budget cuts by conservatives in Congress, there has not been anything like the coherent and effective refashioning that has taken place in the UK. To be sure, the British experience has had its critics. The new leadership of the BBC is often portrayed as abandoning the Reithian tradition and playing too facilely to the marketplace and there are those who think that market forces are destroying the institution in order to save it. What is critical here, however, is that the structure for change, not immunity, has been set in motion and the consequence is that a far more entrepreneurial, far more globally ambitious and more innovative BBC has emerged.

All this being said, technology and even the structural changes that will maximize the impact of new technologies will not turn America's stepchild of public television into a new and glorious BBC. If anything, the future of the world's public-service entities will become more like the present of its American exemplar. The history of American public television – and the future of public-service television around the world – is one of segmentation and narrowcasting and technology may not change that simple fact. It is important to examine demography and market share. Oddly, because PBS always was a sculpted minority, its audience share has remained more stable than that of many other public-service broadcasters around the world. The problems PBS and America's public television stations have traditionally faced will increasingly be found in its more protected equivalents around the world.

Public-Interest Programming by American Commercial Television

Eli M. Noam[1]

Contents

1. The transformation of American television 146
2. A model of program supply 149
3. Public-interest program offerings by commercial TV 155
4. Viewer preferences for public-interest TV 160
5. Financial resources of commercial public-interest TV 162
6. Public-interest program availability for American
   households: a quantification 166
7. News, commercial TV's major contribution 170
8. Missing public-interest programs 171
9. Conclusion 174

1 I would like to thank Hedahne Chung and Jim Parker for the data analysis and other as-
sistance.

145

Public television must be carefully distinguished from *public-interest* television. Public TV is an institutional system of nonprofit or governmental broadcasting. Its product tends to be public-interest TV programs. These are programs that go beyond pure entertainment and provide a cultural, civic, informational or educational function. However, a public TV broadcaster can also offer content that cannot be counted among public-interest programs, such as sports, and popular music. Conversely, public-interest television is not the exclusive province of public TV institutions. Commercial program providers, too, can offer news, education and culture.

The question which this article addresses is the extent of the public-interest program performance by *commercial* television in America. Because American television, among the world's TV systems, has evolved furthest into a market-driven multichannel arrangement, a look at the impact of such evolution on the performance of commercial television is significant beyond the American borders. Has commercial television contributed programs that might be classified as serving a broader public-interest, beyond entertainment? The answer to that question is important to private strategy and public policy. If commercial TV, in an expanded multichannel environment, were to provide a rich menu of those programs that previously were available only on noncommercial TV, the mission and strategy of public TV would be affected. Some could conclude that public TV has become less needed. Others might conclude that public TV needs to refocus on a new mission. Whichever way one comes out, public TV would be different than in the past.

1. The transformation of American television

In purely theoretical terms, it is impossible to answer the question whether multichannel TV provides more public-interest television programs than a limited TV environment. On the one hand, such a TV system tends to offer more of everything, and hence more of public-interest TV. On the other hand, such a system tends to be more competitive, thereby possibly pushing programs to more sensationalist formats, greater dependence upon advertisers, and lowered production budgets. This will be discussed theoretically and investigated empirically further below. But first, let us examine the institutional setting.

The first three decades of commercial television in the US were characterized by an oligopoly of three national programs: CBS, NBC, and an initially weak ABC. Public broadcasting was a minor, though respected, participant in terms of resources and audiences. Commercial broadcasting consisted of several hundred local stations, either "affiliates" of the three major program networks (a few large stations were owned by them) or "independents," using programming provided by syndicators and others. Local stations' primary program production contribution were local news, public affairs and sports. The public television system was a federation of several hundred independent local stations,[2] some of them state-owned, and funded from a variety of sources, including the federal Corporation for Public Broadcasting (CPB). Programs were produced by stations and distributed nationally by the umbrella Public Broadcasting System (PBS). In terms of institutional complexity, the system has often been compared to the Holy Roman Empire.

On top of this institutional inefficiency, the public system was underfunded relative to other industrialized countries.

Government support for public TV (1993; per capita)	
Canada	$31.05
Japan	$31.02
UK	$38.99
US (federal)	$1.09
US (all sources)	$6.83

Source: Ledbetter, 1997

2 The emphasis on localism was said to have been a strategy by the Nixon Administration to divert the efforts of public TV from national issues to local ones.

The three commercial networks, physically located in close proximity in New York and continuously interacting and cooperating on issues of mutual self-interest, were at once fiercely competitive with each other for audiences and talent. They worked together when the public image of the TV industry was at stake. Thus, they jointly limited, to some extent, sensationalism and violence in programming. As the prime outlets for national advertising, they could also keep advertisers at bay, both by limiting the supply of advertising time and by curbing advertiser influence on program content. Being legally restricted from entertainment program production, the networks set content guidelines on such programs produced by others. They also invested in extensive news operations in order to serve as more than entertainment media, and protected the credibility and independence of their news. Local stations, similarly, established news operations, both because they were profitable and because they generated much influence by providing politicians with their major access to the public.

Commercial broadcasters basically liked public TV because it did not contest advertising dollars, its audiences were small, and it relieved the pressures for quality content obligations on commercial TV. CBS, under its president Frank Stanton, contributed 1 million dollars to PBS' first season.

The commercial system rested on a government-awarded station license, which could, at least in theory, be withdrawn by the Federal Communications Commission (FCC) for misbehavior or inadequate program performance. (The national networks did not require licensing and were largely outside of direct regulation except in their capacity as station owners.) At license renewal time (originally every three years, later five) the license could be challenged by community groups complaining about performance, and by rival applicants proposing to do better.

Given the major financial value of a license, broadcasters protected it by consciously cultivating community goodwill through various forms of program service, and by avoiding controversy and imbalance in programs. This led to cautious, middle-of-the-road programs and behavior.

This was the past. Today, American commercial media have

changed, primarily by adding the distribution capacity of cable television, which reaches over 90 percent of U.S. TV households, and is subscribed to by over 65 percent of them. A large number of these cable systems offer more than 70 channels. Direct broadcast satellites (about 150 channels) and "wireless cable" by microwave transmission (dozens of channels) also offer multichannel packages to several millions of households. And soon, multicast digital signals by regular broadcasters will be added, as will be multicasting on cable, and video transmission over telephone lines and on the Internet. At the same time, many of the regulatory requirements on commercial television were loosened and eliminated, making license challenges more difficult.

What has been the impact of this transformation on television's provision of public-interest programs? To answer this question, we proceed first theoretically and then empirically.

2. A model of program supply

Many people believe that the evolution to a multichannel environment has simply led to "more of the same" – simply to a multiplication of the old type of programming. But the empirical evidence does not support this, nor does economic logic.

Commercial television frequently disappoints those seeking the quality of public-interest TV. This cannot be simply because the medium is commercial. After all, most print publishers and film producers are also profit-oriented, and they turn out many works of high cultural standards (as well as of low ones). The traditional commercial TV system tended to serve popular culture rather than high culture because it was limited in capacity, and therefore served mainly the broad center of the "taste distribution." We can analyze programming choice in a simple model for program supply.

Television programs come in a great variety. Let us assume that they can be ordered along an axis ranging from "low content quality" to "high content quality," with quality in terms of cultural or civic value.[3] Shakespeare's plays would be on the right of the axis, while professional wrestling might be on the left. Any given quality level appeals to a segment of the television viewing audience such that it would designate that particular quality as its first viewing preference. We assume that preferences are distributed normally across the spectrum of program qualities, with a single-peaked distribution as depicted in Figure 1.

Figure 1: Audience distribution and program quality

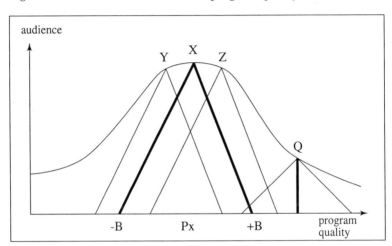

Although viewers prefer a particular program quality level, they are willing to watch programs in a general range B of their first preference, though at a declining rate. B is not infinite; that is, individuals will not view programs that are too distant from their preferred quality level. The audience is represented, in Figure 1, by the triangle bounded by Px+B and X. (We assume no rival channels, for the moment.)

We define the range of public-interest programs as those program quality levels that are higher (to the right) of PQ.

---

3 The "program quality" dimension can be supplemented with many other dimensions. This would add mathematical complexity, but would not enhance the schematic analysis that follows.

Programs are delivered to households by private and public broadcasting organizations. One of the broadcaster's fundamental programming policy decisions is the average quality level P for its programming.

A commercial broadcaster X, wishing maximizing advertising revenue, which in turn means – to simplify – to maximize the audience. It is clear from Figure 1 that the maximum area is reached at the peak of the distribution curve.

Suppose now that other commercial channels are added. A second and third commercial broadcaster Y and Z will position themselves relative to an incumbent broadcaster X so as to maximize audiences, too. The decision rule for a choice of program quality levels Py and Pz, given Px, then is to maximize their audience triangle defined by Py and Pz, minus a prorated share of the area of overlap, in which they share audiences equally.

Y and Z settle in an equilibrium at opposite sides of the peak of the distribution. In other words, they do not quite have the same quality pitch. Much of the conventional interpretation of television sees commercial broadcasting as inherently striving for identical and "lowest common denominators." However, one can see from the model that some differentiation, and a focus on centrist viewers rather than on the "lowest common denominator," is the rational policy.

The addition of further broadcast stations repeats the process, placing stations across the audience preference distribution. As the process continues, the total range of quality levels widens, approaching PQ or even surpassing it if enough channels are added. As more stations are added, the spread of commercial offerings moves (rightward) toward higher quality. But it also moves leftward toward the lower-quality offerings. At the same time, the spacing between chosen program pitches also decreases, as new stations squeeze themselves between existing ones. This means that program channels become more specialized "narrowcasters." The inclusion of an audience's income as a factor that is valued by advertisers is likely to lead to a somewhat greater expansion toward higher quality, if income is associated with education and with preference for higher program quality.

Because of such spread to a broader range of quality options with greater capacity, it would be a mistake to restrict commercial TV to a few channels. Where only a few channels exist, they will serve middle-brow programs. Where many channels exist, they will spread to serve high-quality (as well as low-quality) programs. Less of commercial TV means therefore lower quality programs.

Still, it may take a large number of additional channels in a market system to reach the program quality PQ. This may create the impetus to create or maintain regulatory or public ownership solutions as a shortcut to assure the provision of quality programs. There are several possible approaches:

Regulatory mandates on broadcasters
Government regulations may require each commercial station to devote part of its broadcasting time to programs of pitch PQ or higher. The latter policy was imbedded in the U.S. licensing requirement to provide programs that deal with issues of concern to the community, and by expectations to offer quality children's programs of educational value.

Structural ownership rules
For example, if private broadcasters could program several channels rather than only one as in the past, the spread of their offerings would grow, because they would not want to simply duplicate their own other channels. Instead, they would try to attract new audiences. In the extreme, with a private multichannel monopoly, the quality spread could be quite wide. Of course, this would raise serious issues of media power and of *source* diversity of programs, even as *program* diversity increases.

Pay models for TV
If channel providers can sell "TV-tickets" through subscriptions it might serve quality level PQ if the audience is willing to make up in price what it lacks in numbers.

Creation of public TV stations
A government may set up a channel Q with the mission to have an outlying pitch PQ (see Figure 1). This would mean the creation of a broadcasting system that sets a program policy that is different from the pure commercial approach and contains enough insulation to pursue other optimization goals other than audience maximization. This approach for public broadcasting would be one of the "complementarity" approach in programming.

Several observations can be made about the interrelationship of public and private quality levels:

- In a limited TV channel environment, the support of a public channel is less intrusive than the options of regulatory mandates or structural ownership. And it is more equitable in income terms than the pay-TV option.
- Looking at the model, one can observe that one sideeffect of a high-quality public channel Q is, paradoxically, to push commercial stations somewhat back toward *lower*-quality programs. That is, if a commercial channel might have edged towards high quality PQ, the existence of a public station already serving that audience reduces the commercial incentives to locate there. Hence, a casual comparison of the observed quality differential between commercial and public channels will overstate the difference in their program quality.
- Similarly, the introduction of commercial television channels that compete with a previously monopolistic public channel does not necessarily push the public station to lower quality. Commercial stations edging towards quality offerings would push a public station actually toward *higher*-quality programs. Hence, an increased number of commercial offerings can raise the program quality of a public station, too.

So far, we did not consider cost. Adding program channels may not be economically feasible. Suppose, for the moment, that the programming cost for each program channel is the same, regardless of quality level.

153

Figure 2: Range of feasible quality levels

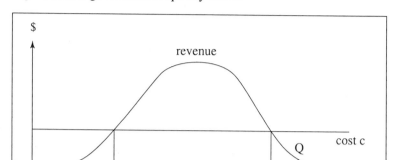

In Figure 2, program cost at each quality level is represented by the horizontal line C. If each audience represents equal worth in terms of advertising revenues, with a constant CPM "cost per thousand" advertising charge, revenues are also distributed normally. The bell-shaped curve represents revenues for a single channel. Together, the two curves define the range of economically feasible quality levels as the range between the intersection points of cost and revenues. It is possible that the desired public-interest quality PQ is outside this range, and that it would hence not be offered by an advertising-based broadcaster even where there are no limits on the number of channels. This might be mitigated in several ways:

– If the high program-quality audiences are more highly valued by broadcasters than low program-quality audiences (because their income might be higher), the revenue curve tilts upward on the right around its peak, resulting in the feasibility range shifting to the right of PR, possibly reaching PQ.

– If high-quality programs are cheaper to produce than mass-culture ones, the cost line tilts similarly downwards on the right and shifts the feasibility range toward higher quality, to the right of PR. (The opposite is the case if high-quality programs are more expensive to produce.)

- The emergence of new distribution technologies shifts the cost line down by reducing distribution costs, shifting PR to the right, and increasing the range of commercially feasible quality.
- New sources of revenue are created that change the shape of the revenue curve and "stretch" it towards PQ. This means various forms of subscription and of pay TV. Outlying program preferences held only by small audiences could then be satisfied if the demand is sufficiently price inelastic. In such a media environment, the higher taste preferences are better served than before, by permitting the often superior economic position of their holders to make itself felt. On the other hand, such a system creates inequalities.
- Government subsidies encourage commercial supply of programs at or near PQ by lowering the cost line in that neighborhood.

To conclude: Commercial providers of television would supply high-quality programs provided the number of channels is large enough. In some cases, it would be necessary to create funding mechanisms that go beyond traditional theoretical advertiser support. But there is no reason to believe, as some critics of private TV do, that the multichannel environment is nothing but "more of the same." Or, as in Bruce Springsteen's song, that there are "fifty-seven channels and nothing on."

3. Public-interest program offerings by commercial TV

After this theoretical discussion, we can look at the empirical evidence. When commercial TV in the US was limited to a handful of channels, network programming was indeed centrist in orientation. Entertainment programs generally had cheerful conclusions to problems, avoided themes that would antagonize major audience segments, and were action-based to attract young audiences. They also had fairly high production budgets in order to attract viewers with a polished product. Few programs were imported since even a slight reduction in attraction to American mass audiences was costly in terms of foregone advertising earnings. There was little program-ming for the intellectual elite, but not much programming aimed at the bottom of the educational and income scale, either. Both of these constituencies were supposed to be served by the public broadcast-ing system, which had a difficult time in reconciling its two conflict-ing program missions, and which opted to primarily serve high-end programs.

This limited TV environment changed radically. Between 1960 and 1996, the number of commercial television stations in America more than doubled, from 515 to 1181. (Public stations grew even more rapidly, from 44 in 1960 to 185 in 1970, 277 in 1980, and 363 in 1996.) Low-power TV station licenses increased from zero to one thousand. All this created the foundation for additional distribution. A fourth commercial broadcast network, Fox, emerged, targeting in particular young audiences attractive to advertisers. Several smaller broadcasting networks were also entered, with varying success.

The main venue of program diversification was cable television, with its growing reach and channel capacity.

Figure 3: Cable TV channel capacity [4]

Channel capacity	1976	1987	1990	1993	1996
54 and over	0 %	15.1	24.4	38.4	47.9
30 to 53	0 %	63.2	66.4	58.2	49.5
20 to 29	12.0 %	14.3	7.4	2.7	2.0
13 to 19	11.9 %	1.3	0.4	0.2	0.2
12 or less	76.1 %	6.1	1.4	0.5	0.4
Avg. channels	14.0 %	39.0	43.0	47.0	53.0

Cable TV developed its own commercial programming channels to differentiate itself from free-broadcast TV and to generate the new income streams of pay-TV. Its advantage is not merely a large num-

---

4 Sources: 1. Sterling, Christopher H. and Kittross, John M., *Stay Tuned: a Concise History of American Broadcasting,* Second Edition, Wadsworth Publishing Company, Belmont California, 1990, p. 660; 2. National Cable Television Association, *Cable Television Devel-opments, Spring 1996.*

ber of channels but also a difference in economic foundation. By being both advertiser and viewer-supported (through cable subscriptions), cable TV is able to afford more specialized "narrowcasting" channels. Viewer preferences could be expressed by their willingness to buy, in effect, tickets for basic and premium program channels.

Traditional public TV was largely missing from the emerging, and extraordinarily dynamic, phase of reshaping American television.[5] In the private sector, new program channels emerged, often vertically integrated by ownership to the cable distribution companies. Most new channels were format-based. They provide all-sports, all-news, all-movies, all-religion, all-cartoons, all-science fiction, all-comedy, etc., around the clock. In 1998, over 100 different cable channels are operating.

Many of these formats were merely an expansion of traditional program categories. Even so, this did not mean, simply more of the same. In any medium, format affects content, and TV is no exception. The 24-hour *CNN* news format permits covering breaking stories in greater depth and length. Examples are the Gulf War, the Clarence Thomas Senate confirmation hearings, disasters such as the San Francisco and Los Angeles earthquakes, and the World Trade Center bombings in New York. In sports, the greater availability of air time led to the coverage of national sports by ESPN, regional sports by regional channels such as *Madison Square Garden*, and specialized channels like the *Golf Channel*. For movies, the absence of most regulatory restrictions, coupled with a need to provide audiences with new alternatives, led to the showing of more sexually explicit and violent programs by some channels.

A second type of new channel took up traditional but more marginal program categories and gave them visibility and presence. Religious programming is an example. (Here, the initiative was taken by the more fundamentalist ministries, such as on the *700 Club*, leaving the mainstream churches behind.) *The Discovery Channel* offers nature documentaries. *The Weather Channel* provides signifi-

---

5 Other noncommercial channels emerged, however, primarily community public access, and municipal channels.

cantly more detailed information to specialized users such as farmers, boaters, or pilots. *The Travel Channel* informs about geography and tourist destinations. *CNBC* provides business information and talk shows. *MSNBC* provides news and interactive links with sites on the Internet.

In addition, multichannel cable also spawned program categories that were new or nearly new to commercial TV. All-music channels for rock, country, and black music emerged, such as *MTV*, *VH-1*, *Black Entertainment Television*, the *Nashville Network*, and *Country Music Television*. *Court TV* entered to cover legal proceedings live, based on the opening of many American court rooms to cameras. *C-SPAN* covers the proceedings of Congress as well as public-affairs events. *Galavision* and other channels provide Spanish-language programs. Other ethnic programming is provided for Japanese, Greek, Hebrew, Italian, Indian, Korean, and other language and cultural groups. *Lifetime* serves mature women. Cultural programs are served by *Arts & Entertainment*, and by *Bravo*. Several shopping channels promote, non-stop, various types of merchandising. The *Learning Channel* provides documentaries.

In this diversity of channels, the channels offering programs which can be categorized primarily as in the categories of *news, culture, education, and information* include the following:

Figure 4: Cable channels providing public-interest programs

Animal World	Fox News Channel
Arts & Entertainment	History Channel
Bravo	Home and Garden Channel
C-Span I	Learning Channel
C-Span II	Mind Extension
CNBC	MSNBC
CNN/CNN Headline News	Nickelodeon
Court TV	Regional News Networks (various)
Disney	The History Channel
Discovery	Travel Channel
Faith and Values	Weather Channel

In addition, several channels are aimed at serving ethnic minorities, not necessarily with public-interest programs:

Black Entertainment Television
Galavision
KBS Television
Univision

The offerings of new cable program networks have increased in recent years. Whereas in 1992, 20 new program channels were concretely proposed or offered to the cable operators, in 1993 it was over 40, and in 1994 over 70. These include many concepts that could not be considered part of public-interest programming, such as channels for dating, games, sports, and entertainment. But others were in the public-interest category, or have the potential to be:

Figure 5: Proposals (for 1996) of channels aimed at public-interest TV programs:

arts performances	inspiration
books	international business
business	jazz
computers	lectures
classic arts	military
deaf and disabled	museums and exhibition
environment; healing	mothers of newborns
health; history	movies; multiculture
do-it-yourself	public affairs
human development	recovery for alcoholics
independent films	Spanish-language programs

This list is impressive, but must be kept in mind that many of these channels might never materialize or make it in the marketplace. Bottlenecks exist due to: (a) insufficient channel capacity; (b) economic infeasibility; and (c) the reluctance of some cable distribution systems to add new channels that compete with their own channels.

4. Viewer preferences for public-interest TV

As cable TV channels emerge that offer public-interest programs, the next question is the extent of their audience popularity.

The new channels compete for audiences with public TV stations. In 1987, according to one study of audience preferences,[6] cable subscribers still indicated that they greatly preferred the public TV programs in a head-to-head comparison over the programs of four specialized cable channels. They preferred public TV for children programs over those of *Disney*; for nature/science over *Discovery*; and for symphony/opera over programs on *Arts & Entertainment*. The exception was for news/discussion, where the commercial *CNN* was more highly valued than public TV. By 1990, however, *Discovery* and *Disney* became the preferred choice. Only in symphony/opera did public TV maintain its lead over *Arts & Entertainment*. In 1990, an audience survey confirmed that "the public perception, commercial specialized channels were seen as substitutes to public TV."[7]

The audiences and reach of cable channels is provided in Figure 6.

These audiences are small, but they add up. For the channels in the public-interest program category, they add up to about 6 percent. While this is not huge, it is about three times as large as public TV audiences have been, which have hovered around 2 percent for years and have inched up to 2.3 percent in 1996.

---

6 Boston Consulting Group, *Strategies for Public Television in a Multi-Channel Environment*, Corporation for Public Broadcasting, March 1991, p 6.
7 See Richard Somerset-Ward in this volume, citing Robert Ottenhoff, COO of PBS, in describing conclusions of a Total Research Corporation survey.

Figure 6: Reach & prime-time audience share of
basic cable Networks[8]

	1996 Reach		Prime Time % of TV HHs			
Cable Network	Mil. HHs	% of TV HHs	1987[9]	1991[10]	1995[11]	1996
A&E	45.5	65	0.2 %*	0.4 %	0.7 %	0.7 %
AMC**	55.0	57			0.2 %	
Animal World**			0.1 %	0.2 %		
BET	32.2	46			0.1 %	0.1 %
Bravo**	22.0	23		0.1 %		
Carto on**	22.0	23	0.3 %	0.5 %	0.6 %	
CMT	23.1	33			0.1 %	0.1 %
CNBC	40.6	58		0.2 %		
CNN**	67.1	70	0.3 %	0.5 %	0.8 %	
CNN* *	58.9	61	0.6 %	0.2 %	0.2 %	0.2 %
Headline News						
Comedy Central	27.3	39			0.1 %	
Court TV	19.6	28			0.1 %	
C-Span**	64.5	67				
C-Span 2**	41.5	43				0.1 %
Discovery	47.6	68		0.6 %	0.8 %	0.8 %
ESPN	48.3	69	1.3 %	1.0 %	0.9 %	
ESPN2**	26.2	27				
E!	24.5	35			0.1 %	
Faith & Values**	24.1	25			0.1 %	0.1 %
Family Channel	45.5	65		0.4 %	0.6 %	
Food Channel**	13.9	14				
Fox News Channel**					0.1 %	
fX**	24.0	25			0.1 %	
Galavision**	5.1	5				0.1 %
History Channel**	8.0	8			0.1 %	0.1 %
HSN**	45.3	47				
Lifetime	45.5	65	0.3 %	0.7 %	0.9 %	

8 Source: Meeker, Mary. "The Internet Advertising Report," *Internet Quarterly: The Business of the Web*, December 1996, Chapter 3, p. 14. Estimated numbers.
9 "Cable Network Numbers on the Rise," *Broadcasting*, January 9, 1989, p. 96, Source: Nielsen Ratings.
10 *Broadcasting*, July 13, 1992, p. 24.
11 Brown, Rich, "TNT Tops Prime Time for 2nd Quarter," *Broadcasting & Cable*, July 3, 1995, p. 20.

	1996 Reach		Prime Time % of TV HHs			
Cable Network	Mil. HHs	% of TV HHs	1987	1991	1995	1996
Learning Channel**	42.4	44		0.2 %	0.3 %	
Mind Extension**	26.0	27			0.1 %	
MSNBC**						0.1 %
MTV	44.8	64		0.3 %*	0.4 %	0.4 %
Nashville**	64.1	67		0.5 %	0.7 %	0.6 %
Network						
Nickelodeon	46.9	67		0.4%*	0.6%	1.0%
Nostalgia	7.7	11				
Prevue	21.0	30			0.1%	
QVC**	53.1	55				
Sci-Fi	18.9	27			0.1%	
TBS	47.6	68		1.3%	1.1%	1.3%
TNT	46.9	67		0.6%	1.1%	1.6%
Travel Channel	14.7	21				0.1%
USA	47.6	68	0.8%	1.1%	1.5%	
VH1	38.5	55		0.1%*	0.1%	0.2%
TWC**	60.7	63		0.1%*	0.1%	
WGN**	39.4	41			0.4%	0.4%

* = Full-day share used for these figures, as prime-time share was not measured by Nielsen
** = 1995 Numbers (Source: Nielsen Media Research)

5. Financial resources of commercial public-interest TV

The strength of the commercial channels lies in the financial resources they can apply to programs. Figure 7 indicates the advertising revenues of the seven cable channels providing public-interest programming. Their advertising revenues exceeded $1.2 billion dollars in 1996. This figure does not include most of the smaller channels, such as *Court TV*, *Bravo*, *History*, *Animal World*, *MSNBC* and *Travel*. If the audience shares for these channels are prorated, another $300 million of advertising would be added. *The Disney Channel*, which is partly a pay channel and partly advertiser-supported, has a 1996 budget of $220 million. In total, advertising support for those public interest-oriented channels can be estimated as $1.6 billion in 1997. On top of that, channels have another revenue stream. Cable distribution networks make payments to many channels (see Figure 8). The average payments range from a high of 41 cents (TNT) and 39 cents (Headline News) to a low of 5 cents (The Weather Channel) and 2 cents (Sci-Fi and VH-1). They are, on average, 21 cents per subscriber/month/ channel. Prorating the channels' reach and ratings for those channels serving public-interest programs (Figure 6) listed in Figure 4, we estimate payments of $800 million. Thus, the overall revenues of commercial public-interest channels are about $2.4 billion and rising. In comparison, the overall budget of the public broadcasting system (excluding public access and municipal cable channels) is about $1.9 billion in 1997 and stable.

These financial resources translate themselves into program investments. The chart below (Figure 8) shows the amounts spent by five specialized cable networks on several specialty programming types, and compares this with expenditures by the public TV system on the same program categories.

Figure 7: Basic cable networks: 1986–1996 advertising ($mil)[12]

Network	Unit	1985	1987	1990	1993	1996
CNN	$	70	111	221	269	343
Nickelodeon	$	10	27	69	182	313
Discovery	$	1	6	46	120	211
Learning	$	0	4	9	18	61
A&E	$	6	14	49	112	179
CNBC	$	0	0	23	58	110
Weather Channel	$	8	11	20	34	55
Total		95	173	427	793	1,432

12 Sources: Meeker, Mary, *Morgan Stanley: The Internet Advertising Report*, Harper Business: New York, 1996, Table 3–10, and Paul Kagan and Associates.

Figure 8: Programming networks, subscribers, and license fees[13]

Network	List License Fees (per sub/per month)	Average License Fee (per sub/per month)
A&E	0.27	0.09
BET	0.1	0.07
CNBC	0.17	0.08
CNN	0.38	0.27
COM	0.14	0.07
COURT TV	0.12	0.06
DSC	0.15	0.12
E!	0.09	0.06
ESPN	0.65	0.6
FAM	0.17	0.09
HN	0.38	0.39
LIFE	0.16	0.09
MTV	0.32	0.12
NICK	0.37	0.15
SCI-FI	0.05	0.02
TLC	0.09	0.04
TNN	0.3	0.12
TNT	0.43	0.41
OON	0.15	0.07
TWC	0.1	0.05
USA	0.29	0.22
VH-1		0.1

Figure 9: Program expenditures[14]

Cable Channel	1990	1992	1996
Nickelodeon	54.0	77.0	244.0
Arts and Entertainment	38.4	57.2	140.3
The Discovery Channel	38.0	75.0	174.4
Disney		120.0	220.0
The Learning Channel	3.5	8.5	32.2

13 Source: *Economics of Basic Cable Networks*, Paul Kagen Associates, Inc. (1994). As quoted in "Horizontal Concentration and Vertical Integration in the Cable Television Industry," *Review of Industrial Organization*, 12: 501 – 508, 1997.
14 Paul Kagen Associates – quoted in PBS Economic Analysis, March 1992.

Figure 10: Spending on programming types – amount spent by PBS and cable services for each of the following types of programming[15] (in millions $)

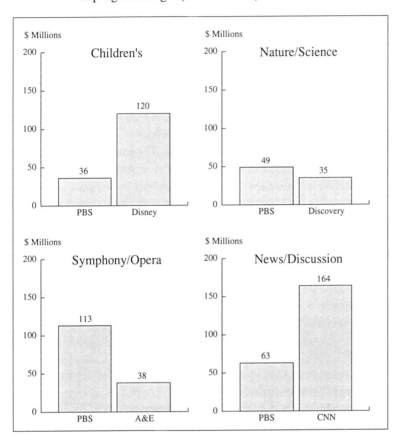

Total PBS: $261 million; total cable (Discovery, CNN, A&E, Disney): $358 million

The charts indicate that *Disney*'s and *CNN*'s audience lead over the public TV system are associated with a greater budget. In contrast,

15 Boston Consulting Group. *Strategies for Public Television in a Multi-channel Environment.* March 1991, p. 7. Source: PBS, BCG.

the public TV budget for symphony/opera was higher, and budgets were about even for nature/science.

It should be noted that the comparison of Figure 9 understates commercial channels' combined resources because it lists only one cable channel in each category, whereas there are multiple cable providers in for category, specialized or more general ones.

The commercial cable channels produce some of these programs themselves, and acquire others. *A&E* developed a strong relationship with the British Broadcasting Corporation, including a right of first refusal for programs. In forging these relationships with foreign public TV producers, American commercial channels benefit from the financial pressures on these public TV providers, which lead them latter to unsentimentally sell their programs to the highest bidder. And even when these programs end up with public TV, their price may be higher due to the presence of the cable channels as bidders in the market.

Of course, money isn't everything. Some fairly low budget productions from PBS have attracted loyal audiences, for example, *The French Chef*, or the *PBS News Hour with Jim Lehrer*. Support for public TV can also be inferred from the doubling of dues-paying membership between 1980 and 1993, to more than 5 million, contributing about $400 million annually.

6. Public-interest program availability for American households: a quantification

The programs available to a typical TV household have tremendously increased in the past decades. It is one thing to state this in general terms, and quite another to quantify it. To do so, we categorize and measure the programs available to TV audiences in New York (Manhattan) during one typical week, over a period of three decades. The dates are 1969 (pre-cable, 10 channels), 1985 (20 channels) and 1997 (77 channels). In the pre-cable era, the region was served by 10 broadcasting channels, while the national weighted average was about 5. In 1985, Manhattan's 20-channel system was actually below the national average. By 1997, New York's 77 channels system was in the upper third of capacity, but by no means at the top. Thus, in terms of commercial offerings, New York is not atypical. Where a difference exists is in the noncommercials offerings. Here, New York has four public TV channels, more than twice the national average. There are four community (public access) channels, about three municipal channels, and one City University channel. Combined, the noncommercial offerings in New York City are about 2–3 times that of the national average.

For purposes of the analysis, we looked at a random week in 1969, 1985, and 1997, and assigned every program shown during that period to various program categories. Excluded were pay-per-view channels and the program guide channels. Also excluded were movies, since the selection of some of them as "public-interest" programs would have to be highly subjective. The assignment to program categories was based on individual programs and not on entire channels. Thus, for example, the sports news and entertainment news programs on CNN were not included in the category "News."

Sources were issues of *TV Guide*, the logs of the public access clearinghouse, the organization MNN, and the program guide for the municipal system Crosswalk. The public affairs channel C-SPAN, though technically nonprofit, is included among commercial channels since it is financed and controlled by the cable TV industry.

The results are listed in Figure 11. For each horizontal category, the top (bold-faced) line represents commercial channel hours, and the lower line (italicized) represents noncommercial hours.

Several observations can be made from the data.

– The number of total program hours has increased phenomenally, from 1 016 in 1969, to 3 431 in 1985, to 9 603 in 1997. This amounts to half a million program hours per year! It constitutes an increase of 845 percent over 28 years, or an annual compound growth rate of 10.83 percent.

– The growth of commercial program hours has been faster than that of noncommercial programs (988 percent vs 243 percent), with annual growth rates of 8.9 percent vs. 4.5 percent.

167

Figure 11: Public-interest TV: commercial and nonprofit
program hours and growth (weekly, Manhattan)

	1969	1985	1997	1969–1985	1985–1987	1969–1997	Compounded Annual Growth
News	55	217	1631	294	651	2865	12.86 %
	14	22	55	57	150	292	5 %
Financial	14	158	335	1028	112	2292	12 %
	3	8	21	166	163	600	7 %
Documentary/	12	27	380	125	1307	3066	13 %
Magazine	10	16	49	600	206	390	5.34 %
Health/	7	83	185	1085	123	2542	12.4 %
Medicine	4	7	42	75	500	950	8.75 %
Science/	8	26	230	223	784	2775	12.7 %
Nature	5	11	14	120	27	220	3.74 %
Cultural	8	15	85	87.5	466	963	8.80 %
	17	28	91	64	225	435	6.17 %
Quality	12	29	94	142	224	683	7.62 %
Children	36	40	98	11	145	716	3.63 %
Education	9	31	112	244	261	1144	9.41 %
	6	14	96	133	585	1500	10.40 %
Religion	14	123	149	778	21	964	8.80 %
	6	12	45	50	275	516	7.45 %
Foreign	29	187	367	544	96	1165	9.48 %
Language	18	26	42	44	61	133	3.07 %
Total Public	168	896	3568	433	298	2023	11.53 %
Int. Programs	119	184	553	54	200	365	5.63 %
Overall	820	3215	8929	262	177	912	8.9 %
Program Hours	196	216	674	61	212	402	4.5 %
Overall Channels	10	20	77	100	285	770	7.55 %

(a) Commercial channels
(b) Noncommercial stations

- The growth of public-interest programming has been extraordinarily high. For noncommercial channels the increase has been 434 hours per week, or 365 percent. It is even higher for commercial TV, where the increase has been 3,400 hours, or 2,203 percent, for an annual growth rate of 11.5 percent.
- Commercial TV's increase in the supply of public-interest TV has been especially high for news, documentary & magazine programs, health/medicine, science/nature, and finance. All of these show annual growth rates of about 12 percent. Somewhat lower growth rates exist for quality children's programs (7.6 percent), religion (8.8 percent), foreign language (9.5 percent), and education (9.4 percent).
- The number of program hours of public-interest programs is especially high for news, which accounts for 46 percent of all commercial public-interest programs. Documentary/magazine account for 10.65 percent, financial 9.4 percent. The share is lower for quality children's programs, with 2.6 percent or 94 weekly hours.[16] For education, it is 3.1 percent. As a share of all hours, not just of public-interest program time, commercial TV's supply of quality children's programs is 1.1 percent, and for education, 1.3 percent.
- Overall, the share of public-interest programming in total program hours almost doubled, from 28.2 percent to 43 percent. For noncommercial TV, it rose from a high of 60.7 percent to an even higher 82 percent. Thus, multichannel competition did not lead to lower quality standards on public TV.
- The number of channels offering primarily public-interest programming is quite large. By our count, there are 18 such commercial channels in New York. There are 3 foreign channels. There are also 11 nonprofit channels, 3 public stations, (3 municipal, 1 City University, 4 public access). This adds up to 32 channels on the cable dial. That dial comprises in theory 77

---

16 The category of "quality children's programs" was the most subjective and hardest to acertain. It is hard to draw the line. A study focusing on children's TV would have to use more detailed information than that available for this article. For now, the children's program quality data should be viewed as orders of magnitude rather than as an exact figure.

channels, practically 74, from which one should exclude the 5 pay-per-view channels, for a real channel count (including pay-TV) of 69. Channels representing nonprofit and public interest-oriented commercial offerings hence account for 46 percent of the cable dial! (But they account for only 8.5 percent of viewership.) Commercial public-interest channels alone account for 30 percent of the dial, accounting for a quarter (26 percent), of all channels, and a third (32 percent), of all English-language commercial channels.

– A final observation: the growth in the number of hours for most categories of public-interest programs has been so large as to make most potential objections to the inclusion of this program or that channel largely irrelevant. Even if one disallowed a full three-quarters of all programs which we counted as belonging to public-interest categories, the increase would be still be a whopping 600 percent!

7. News, commercial TV's major contribution

The greatest contribution of commercial TV to public-interest TV has been in news and public affairs. Multichannel commercial TV has generated vastly more such programming than in the past. In New York, there are 233 hours of news available each day, not counting financial news, entertainment, specialized weather, and interview programs. Some of it is national, such as CNN, Fox News Channel, and MSNBC. One 24-hour news channels is local. Some cable channels run a few hours of foreign-language news for various language minorities, such as in Korean, Chinese, Japanese, Italian, French, Hebrew, and Polish.

Furthermore, the news coverage of traditional local broadcasters has expanded considerably in terms of hours. The reasons are good audience ratings and relatively low production costs. Some of the "local" news is essentially nationally syndicated news that is packaged as local.

On the other hand, with profits squeezed, the budgets of the national commercial news operations of the major networks have been curtailed, after a period of great increase.

Similarly, competition has led news magazine shows to focus more on sensationalist subjects, and the shrill tone of syndicated "tabloid" shows like *Hard Copy, Inside Edition,* or *A Current Affair* has spilled into the more serious news magazine. Yet this pales in comparison to the fact that serious news magazine shows (like *60 Minutes, 20/20, Prime Time Live, 48 Hours, Dateline, Now,* and *Turning Point*) have proliferated (to 14 in 1996) and become popular (four were in the top 20 shows in 1996).

8. Missing public-interest programs

It would be a mistake to draw the policy conclusion that just because many categories of public-interest programs are satisfied by commercial channels, all of them are adequately provided for. The question therefore is which public-interest program categories are *not* being offered by this system. They are not easy to identify. In the future, with hindsight, we may recognize missing categories. Others might be determined by reference to what is available today on video cassettes, the Internet, and public TV. This would include:

Cultural performance programs
There are relatively few programs on commercial TV in the category of cultural performances, especially in comparison to public TV series such as "Masterpiece Theater," "American Playhouse," "Great Performances," "Dance in America," and "Live from Lincoln Center." The cable channel *Bravo* comes closest, but it has moved to focus on quality motion pictures; the *Arts & Entertainment* channel, similarly, has moved more towards documentaries and away from the arts.

Specialized instructional programs

Programs in languages without a geographically concentrated U.S. base of speakers

Foreign channels,
outside of Mexican ones.

Ethnic channels,
outside of Hispanic and African-American ones.

Controversial political programs
There are no commercial TV channels of extreme left-wing or extreme right-wing content, though there are plans for such channels. Some of these programs are available, through nonprofit public-access channels that are local, rather than national, in scope. In general, commercial channels try to avoid giving offense.

Children and education
The main failing of the traditional limited broadcasting system has been in quality programs aimed at children. In the past, the major commercial television networks provided mostly cartoon shows and uninspired fare, and with advertising aimed at very young children. When such an approach proved socially and politically untenable, many broadcasters reduced such children's programming as far as they could without losing so much goodwill that they would jeopardize their license renewal.

Partly in consequence, the public TV system received much support in order to serve children's needs. Top-rated programs for children became *Sesame Street, Barney and Friends, Shining Time Station, Mr. Roger's Neighborhood* and *The Electric Company.*

In principle, there is nothing inherent in commercialism to prevent the provision of quality children's programs. The publishers of quality children's books are mostly commercial firms. The missing element in TV is a funding mechanism that is not advertising-based. Cable television provides, at least in theory, such a link by offering programs to subscribers as a differentiating attraction relative to free broadcasting, and as a special for-pay feature, at the price of income-based inequality of access. This is the theory. And it raises equity issues.

The most successful channel for children is Viacom's *Nickelodeon*, which has 30 percent of the viewing time of 6 – 11 year olds, in contrast to less than 4 percent of ABC and CBS (The NBC network has dropped children's programming altogether). In the process, *Nickelodeon* is doing quite well financially, also adding spin-offs such as a magazine and toys. Its programs, on the whole, are more entertaining than educational, but it also produces "Nick News" hosted by a respected newswoman. Programs for children are also on the *Disney Channel*, and on *USA, Discovery*, ("Ready, Set, Learn") and other commercial cable channels.

For pre-school children, however, there are still very few quality programs on commercial cable channels. There is no "Fairy Tale Channel" or "Elementary School Channel." *Nickelodeon* started a lineup for pre-school kids (Nick Jr.) including four minutes of advertising. The Children's Television Workshop, producers of *Sesame Street,* considered offering programs for commercial channels. The creators inside the organization were split. They wanted to strengthen the quality of TV available to children, but feared denying this to children from households too poor to afford cable TV.

Because this area is underserved by commercial providers, Congress, by law, required broadcasting stations to serve "the educational and informational needs of children." Initially the FCC gave stations considerable latitude in fulfilling this obligation. This flexibility led some broadcasters to count their cartoon programming as serving these needs. Eventually, the FCC made quality children's programs a priority. After considerable political jaw-boning, the industry committed itself "voluntarily" to 3 hours a week of quality children's programs.

Local programs
Almost all commercial public-interest TV programs outside of local news are national rather than local in nature, origin, and distribution.

Programs aimed at the poor
These tend to be uninteresting to advertisers and cable operators.

9. Conclusion

Multichannel television has transformed the nature of audiences. In that process, the public-interest program contribution of commercial TV increased considerably. It provides channels of quality (together with channels of low standards). Its audiences are modest (6 percent) but not trivial, and larger than those of public TV (2.3 percent). Its budgets are higher, $2.1 billion vs. $1.9 billion for the public system. Its hours of programs are large and growing, especially for news.

But this is not to say that a market-based system works fully in the supply of public-interest programs. Some content categories, including quality children's programs, are not commercially offered in a major way. Controversial programs are being avoided. There is therefore still ample room for alternative suppliers such as public TV or other noncommercial systems.

Multichannel TV supports diversity. It also creates problems. Except for unusual events, the electronic hearth around which the entire country used to congregate nightly is no more. But such communal experience of continuous information-sharing was a historical aberration, clashing with a more fragmented media past and a more information-rich future.

Multichannel TV also creates gatekeeper power, if a single firm controls the distribution. It can limit the access to audiences by independent or competing providers of quality programs. Satellite TV and cyber-TV are likely to reduce that problem over time.

There is also the question of affordability. Multichannel TV is not free, and hence burdens the access of some poor population groups to commercially provided public-interest programs.

On the whole, however, the positive program contributions of multichannel TV are impressive. Those who are critical of the performance of the limited commercial television often tend to believe that the less there is of it, the better. Actually the opposite is the case: the most problematic system is a limited but powerful commercial system. Others believe that the high profits of a limited TV system are required for high-quality programs. But that assumes that public-interest programming must be based on a subsidy system in which rich TV institutions pass on some of their resources to public-interest concerns. What the American experience shows is that the provision of public-interest programs by commercial TV can flourish in an environment of many avenues of production and distribution serving numerous tastes. It shows that one can do well by doing good. This trend is likely to continue, and accelerate on a cyber-TV that is based on computer networks and video servers.

It would be myopic to claim that all program needs have already been met by the commercial system. But it would be equally narrow-minded to deny that improvement has taken place.

The Authors

James Ledbetter
is a staff journalist on New York's *Village Voice* where he writes the "Press Clips" column. He has contributed to *The Nation, The Washington Post* and *Mother Jones* among other publications and is author of *Made Possible By ...*, his recent work on public television finance.

Eli M. Noam
is Director of the Columbia Institute for Tele-Information (CITI) at Columbia University in New York and teaches Economics and Finance at the Columbia Business School. His area of expertise comprises electronic media, telecommunications and communications technologies. From 1987–1990 Professor Noam served as Public Service Commissioner for New York State. As the author of numerous books and articles, his renown has spread well beyond academic circles. The Bertelsmann Foundation has published the German version of his book "Cyber-TV. Theses on the Third Television Revolution."

Monroe E. Price
is communications fellow with the Markle Foundation, Danciger Professor of Law at the Benjamin N. Cardozo School of Law, Yeshiva University, New York and founder and co-director of the Oxford Programme in Comparative Media Law and Policy, Wolfson College, Oxford University. He is also Director of Cardozo's Howard M. Squadron Program of Law, Media and Society. His book,

Television, National Identity and the Public Sphere, was published by Oxford University Press. He has served as deputy director of California Indian Legal Services, and was one of the founders of the Native American Rights Fund. He served as dean of Cardozo School of Law from 1982 to 1991. Dean Price was president of California's Foundation for Community Service Cable Television, deputy director of the Sloan Commission on Cable Communications, and is co-author of a treatise on cable television. He was court-appointed referee to monitor the Los Angeles school district's desegregation plan and is on the Board of Directors of the Fund for Modern Courts. He is the author of numerous articles on communications policy, copyright and the arts. He was a member of the Commission on Television Policy at the Carter Presidential Center. He received his B.A., 1960, LL.B., 1964, from Yale University.

Willard D. Rowland, Jr.,
dean of the School of Journalism and Mass Communication at the University of Colorado, Boulder, teaches and conducts research in the history, regulation and policy of American and international broadcasting and telecommunications. He has written and published on the television violence debates, public broadcasting, and the history of journalism and communication studies. He served as director of research and long-range planning for the Public Broadcasting Service. Dr. Rowland is presently chair of the Board of Directors of KBDI-TV, Channel 12 in Denver, and recently served as president of the National Association of Schools of Journalism and Mass Communication. He received a B.A. in history from Stanford, M.A. from the Annenberg School of Communication at the University of Pennsylvania and a Ph.D. from the University of Illinois.

Richard Somerset-Ward
was on the staff of the BBC for 21 years from 1963–1984. His assignments included a spell as the BBC's director in the United States (1976–1978), and as head of Music & Arts Programming for BBC Television (1978–1984). Since 1984, he has been based in New York as an independent producer, writer, and consultant. In 1993, he was the author of the Background Paper for "The Twen-

tieth Century Fund's Task Force on the Future of Public Television" (published under the title *Quality Time?*). He is currently a consultant to the Corporation for Public Broadcasting, for whom he has recently completed a report on "Programming for the Digital Age." His current television productions include a series called The Nation's Pictures (about the collection at the National Gallery of Art in Washington, D.C.) His book *The Story of Opera* will be published in September 1998.

The Editors

Eli M. Noam
is Director of the Columbia Institute for Tele-Information (CITI) at Columbia University in New York and teaches Economics and Finance at the Columbia Business School. His area of expertise comprises electronic media, telecommunications and communications technologies. From 1987–1990 Professor Noam served as Public Service Commissioner for New York State. As the author of numerous books and articles, his renown has spread well beyond academic circles. The Bertelsmann Foundation has published the German version of his book "Cyber-TV. Theses on the Third Television Revolution."

Jens Waltermann
Jens Waltermann completed his first degree after studying law at the Goethe-Universität Frankfurt/Main and international law at the Université de Geneve. After gaining practical experience in commercial litigation and arbitration with the international law firm Baker and McKinsey in Frankfurt, Berlin and Sydney he spent two years from 1995 to 1997 as a McCloy Scholar at the Kennedy School of Government, Harvard University. Jens Waltermann has published articles on corporate, banking and commercial law as well as on communitarianism. He is admitted to practice as an attorney in Frankfurt/Main. Since 1997 he has been with the Bertelsmann Foundation in Germany as Director Media Policy.